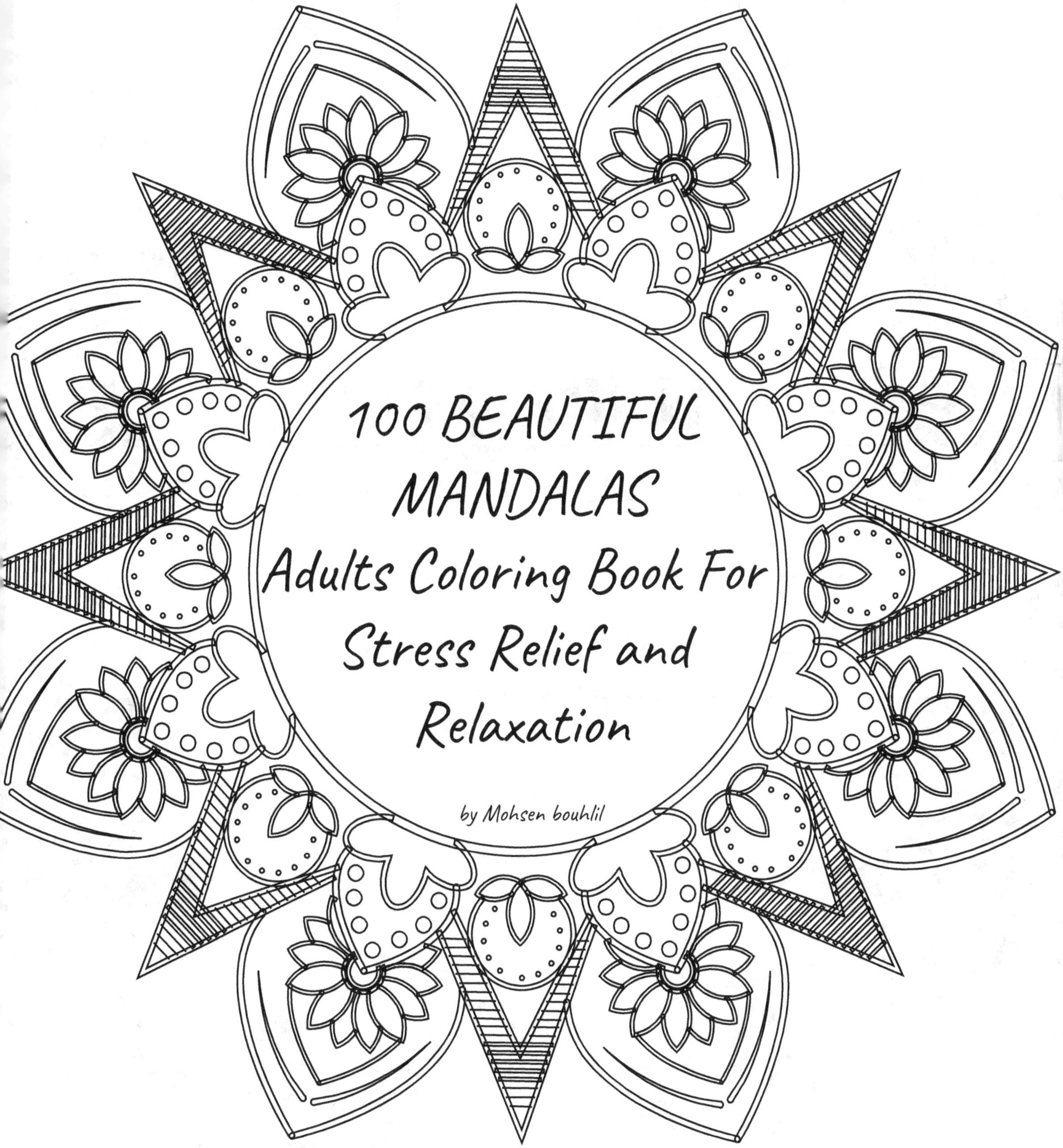

100 BEAUTIFUL MANDALAS
Adults Coloring Book For Stress Relief and Relaxation

by Mohsen bouhlil

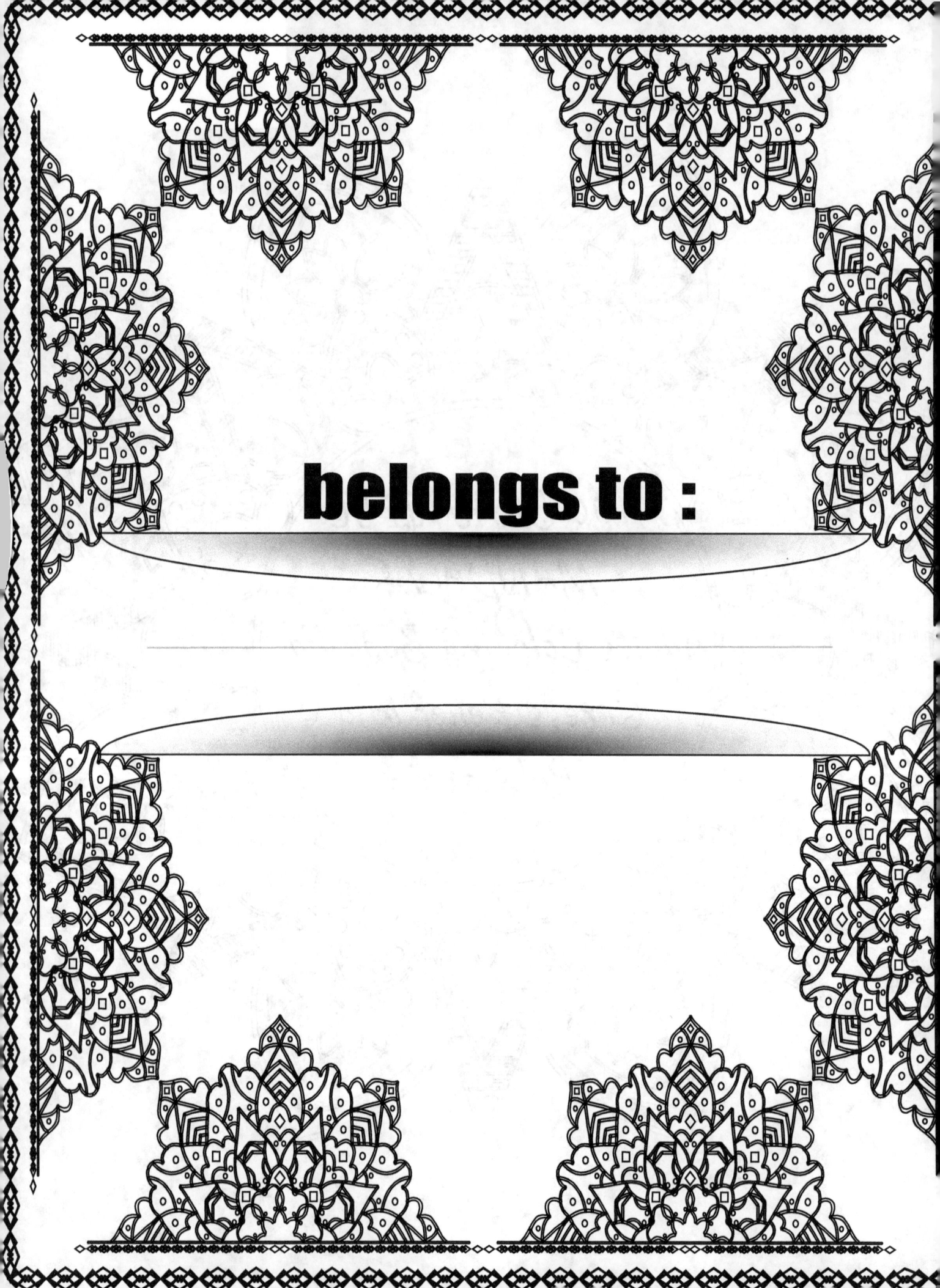

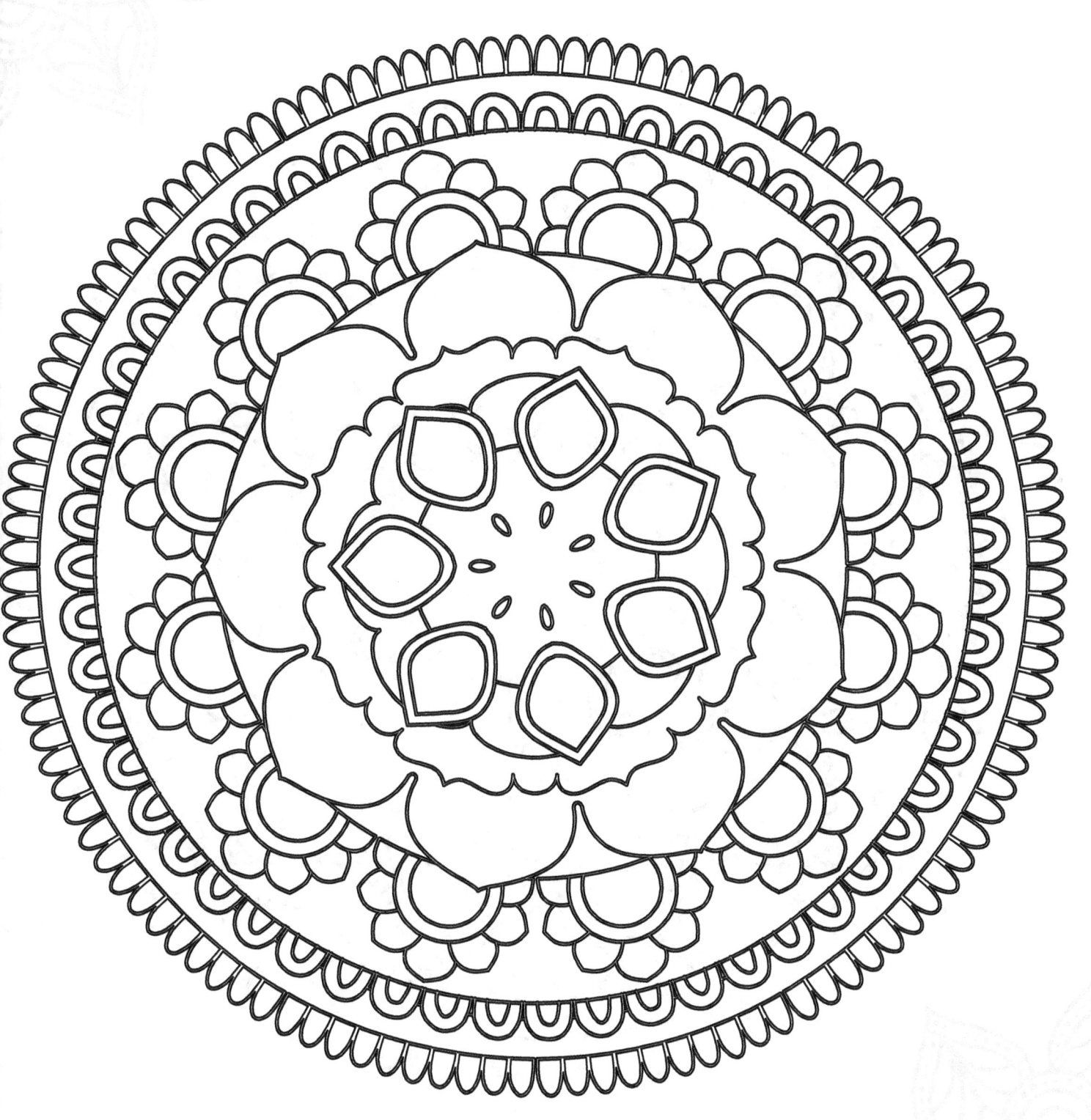

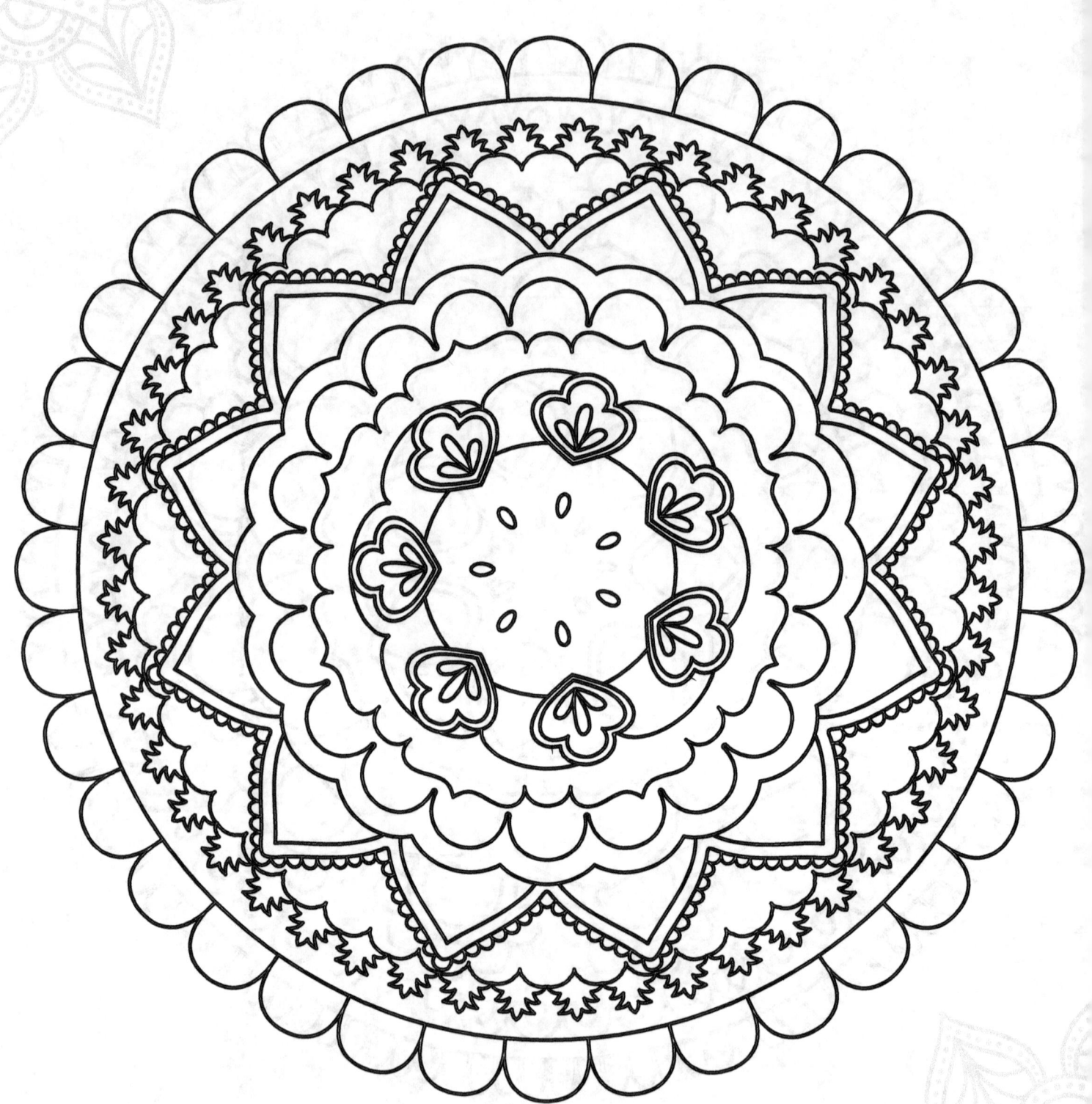

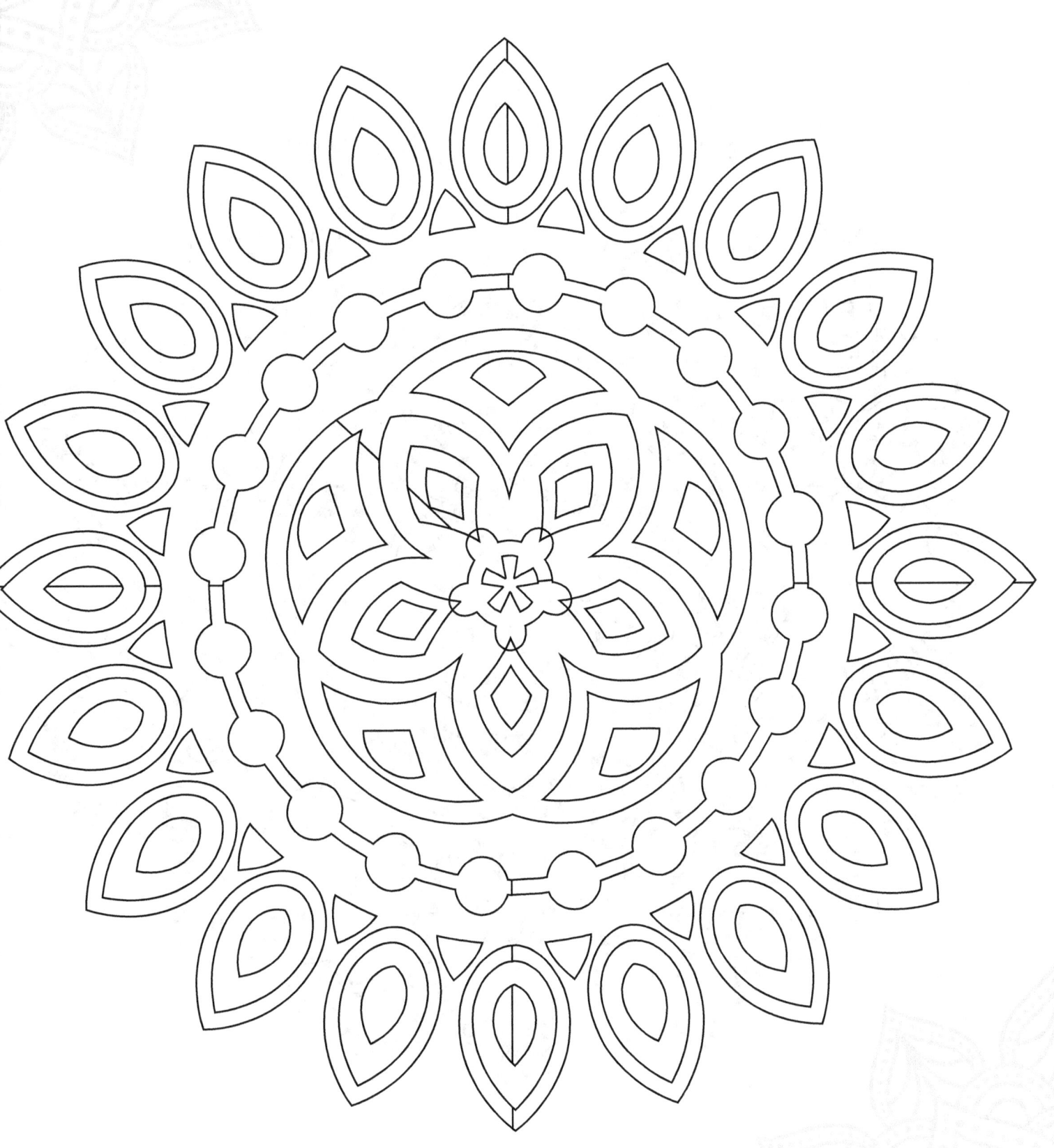

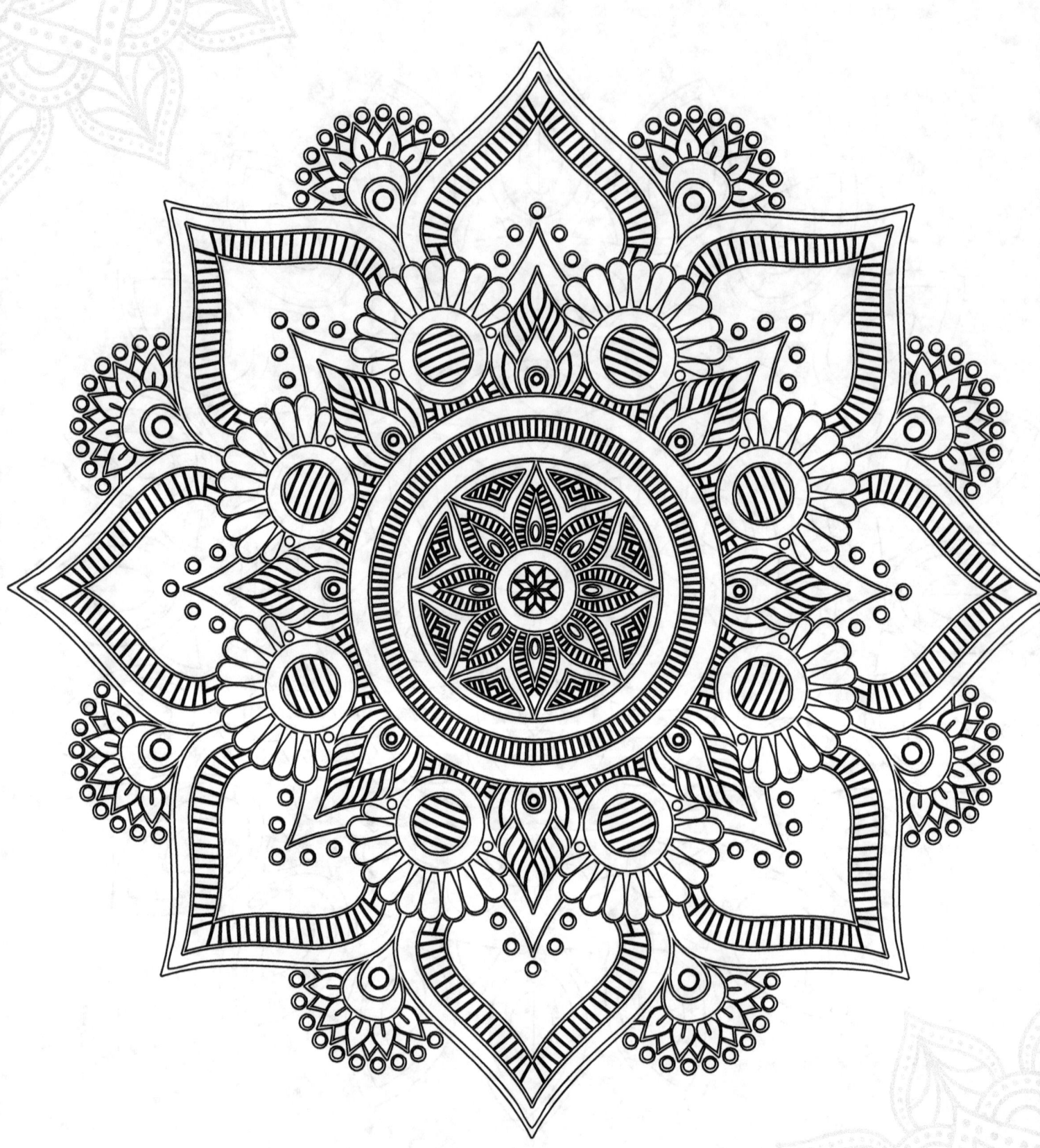

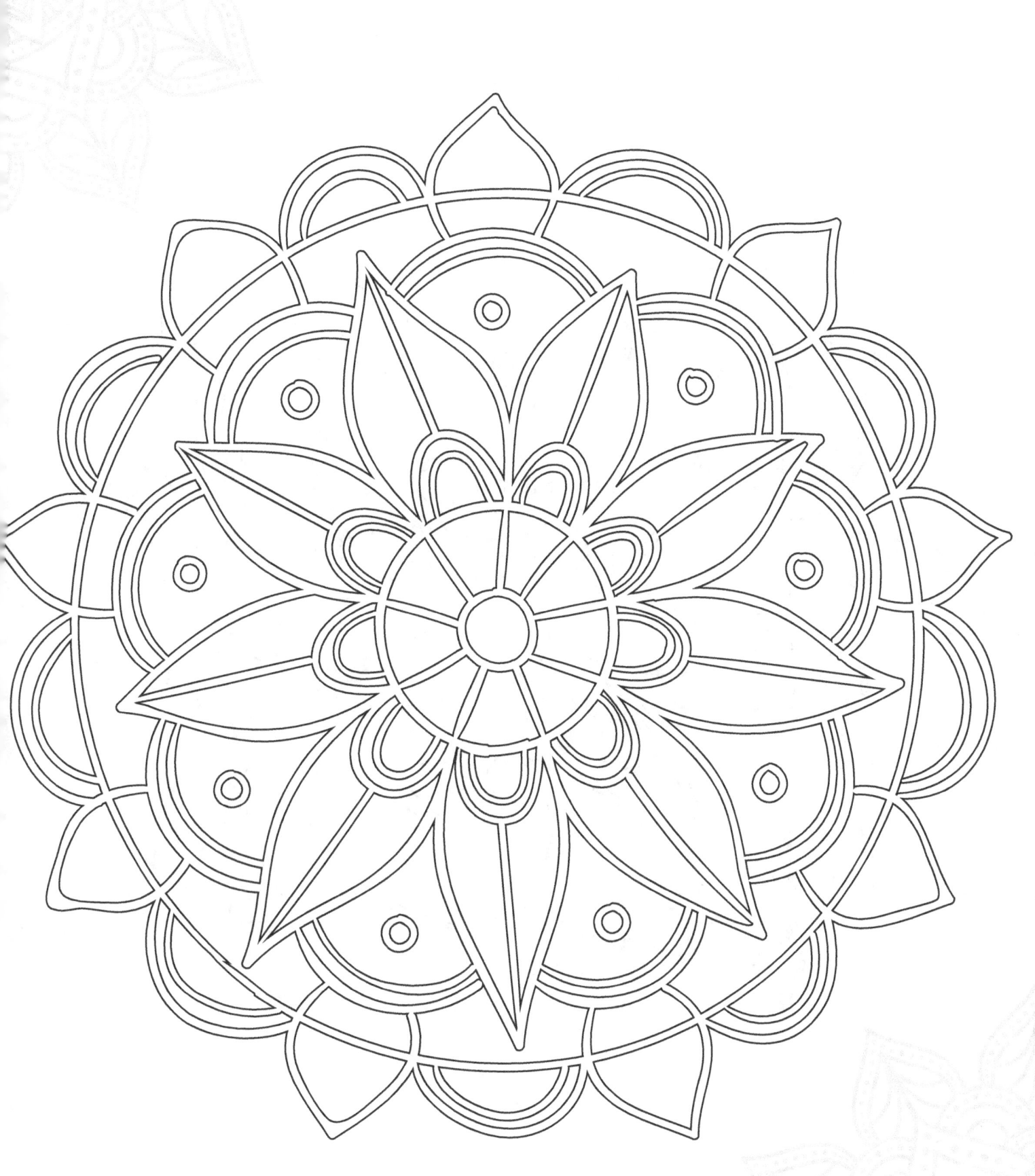

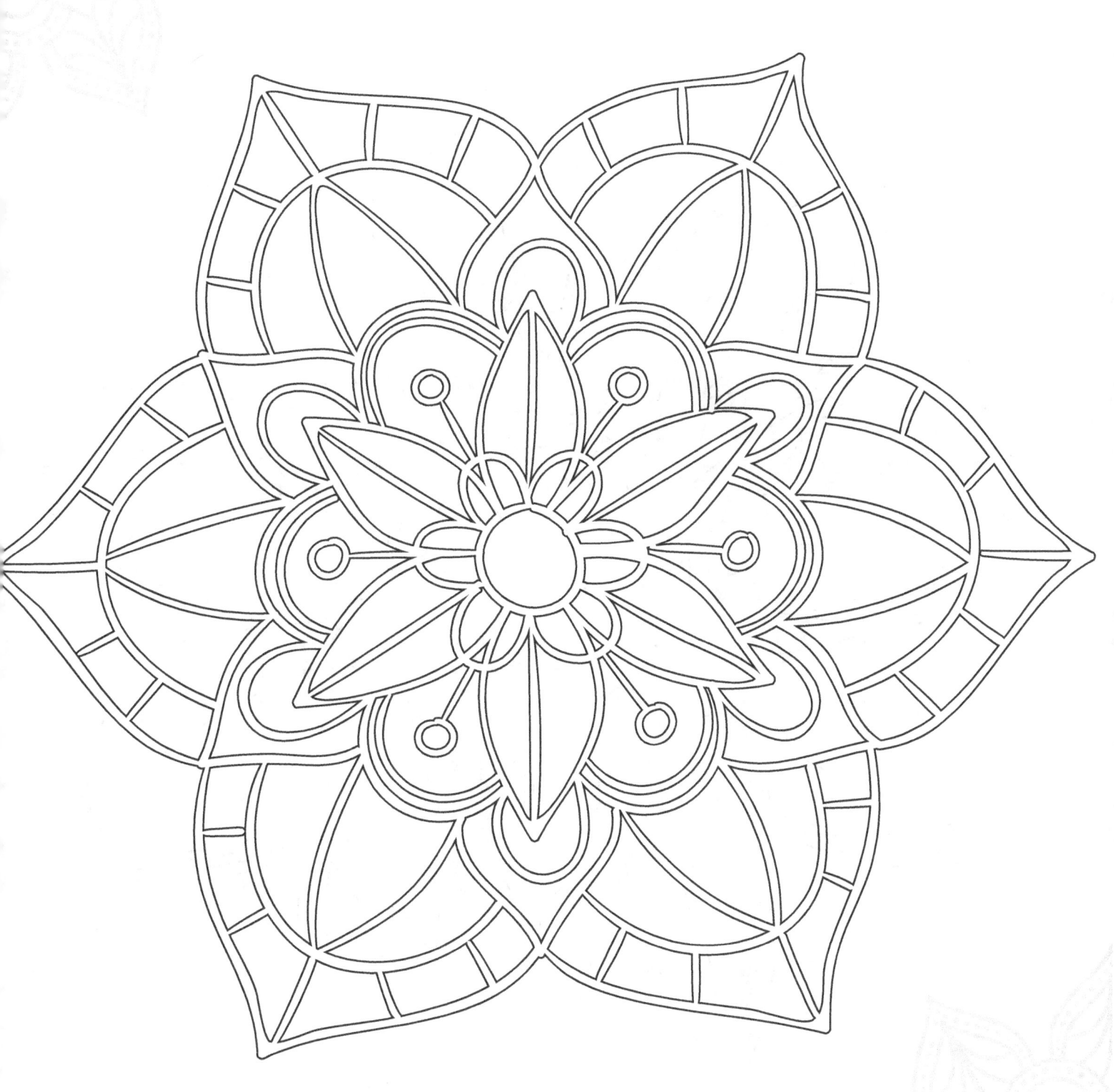

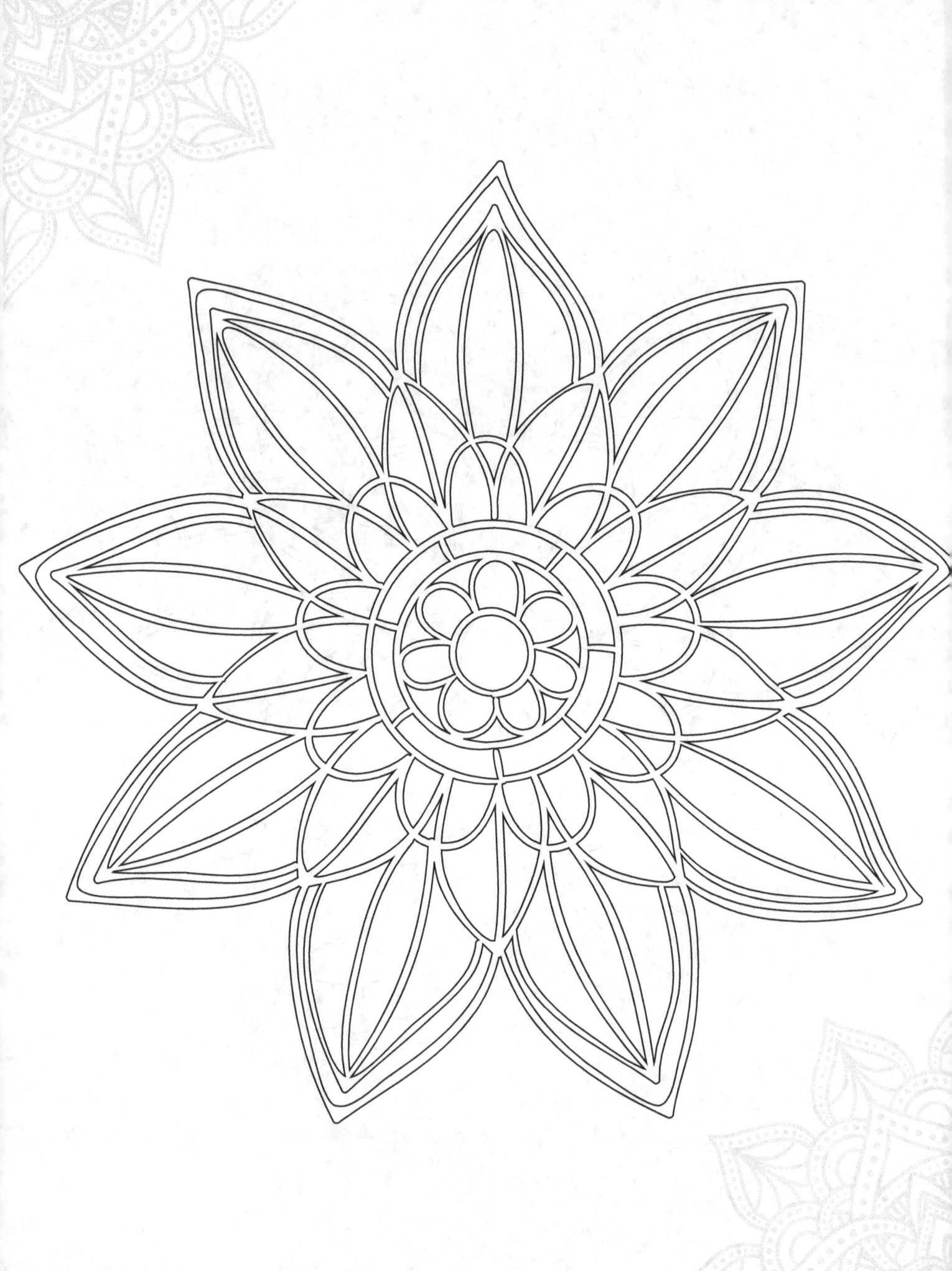

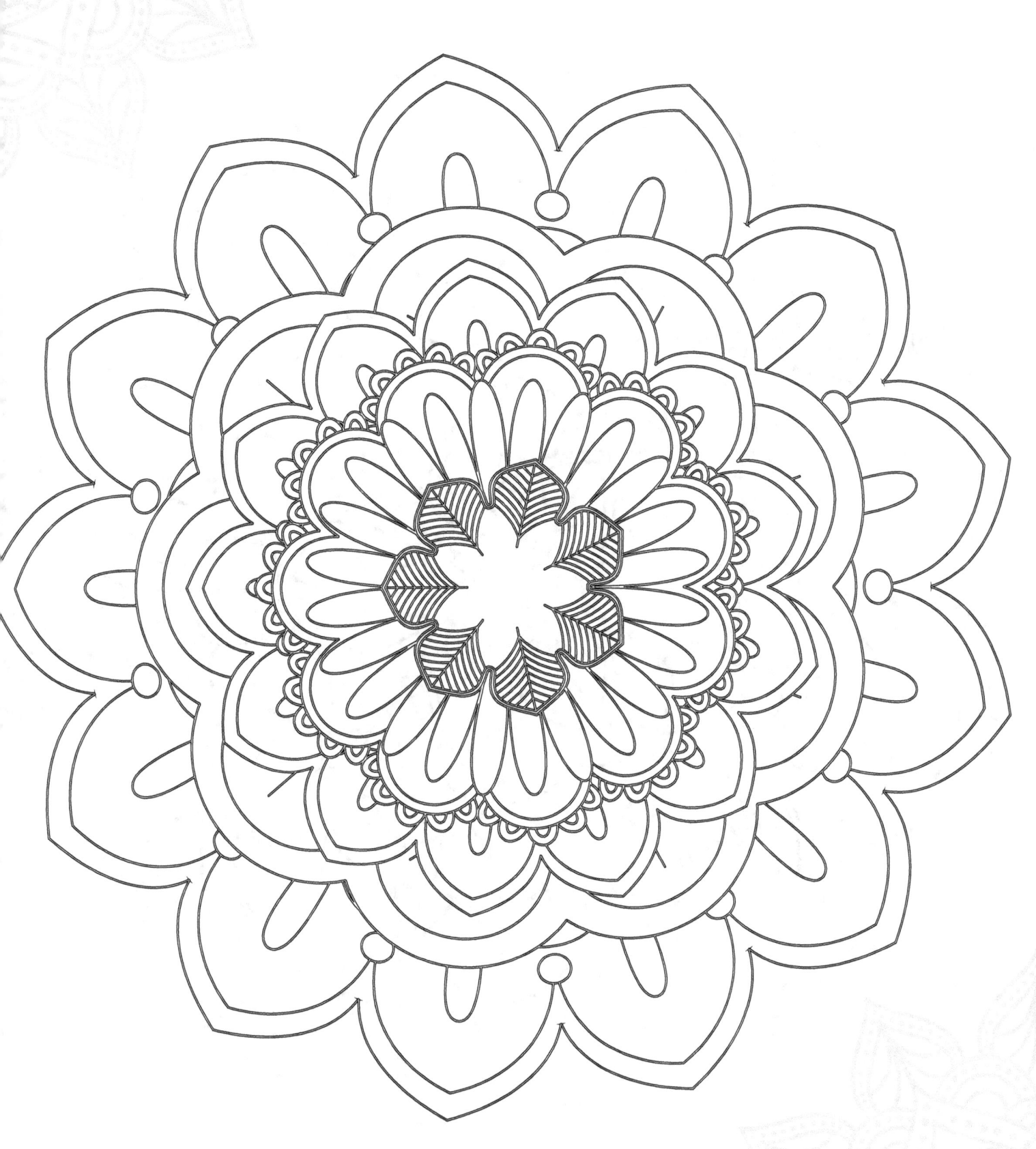

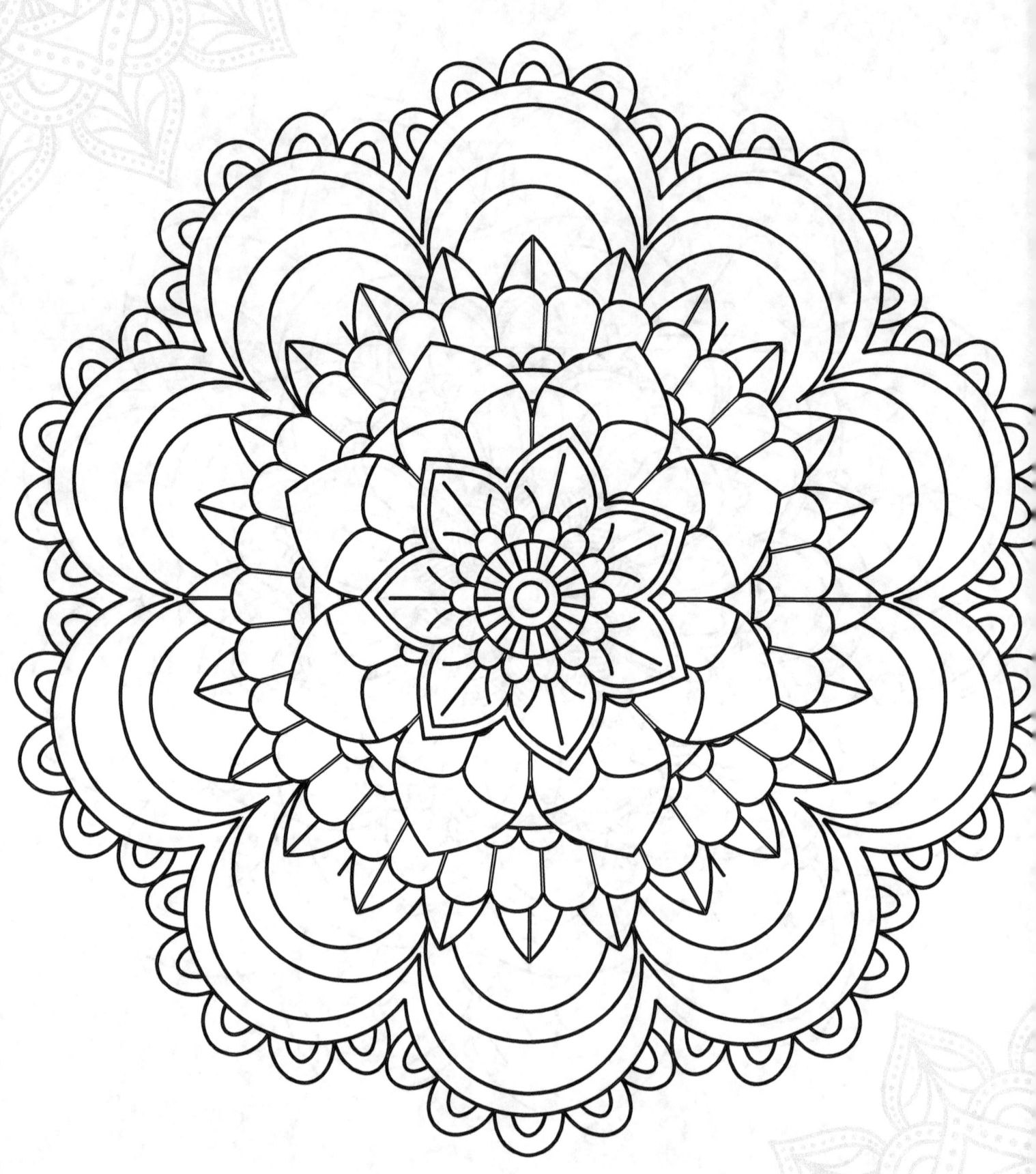

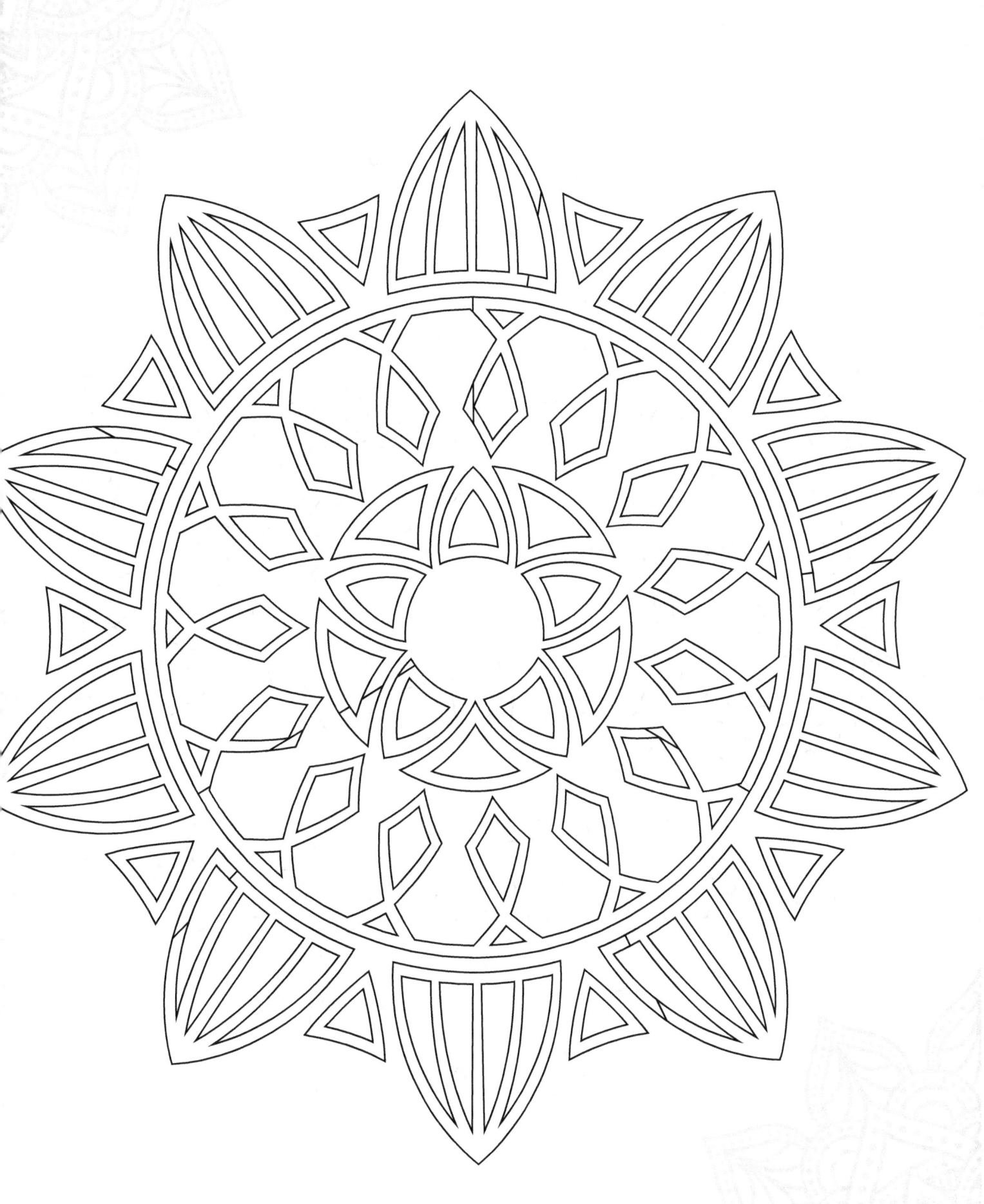

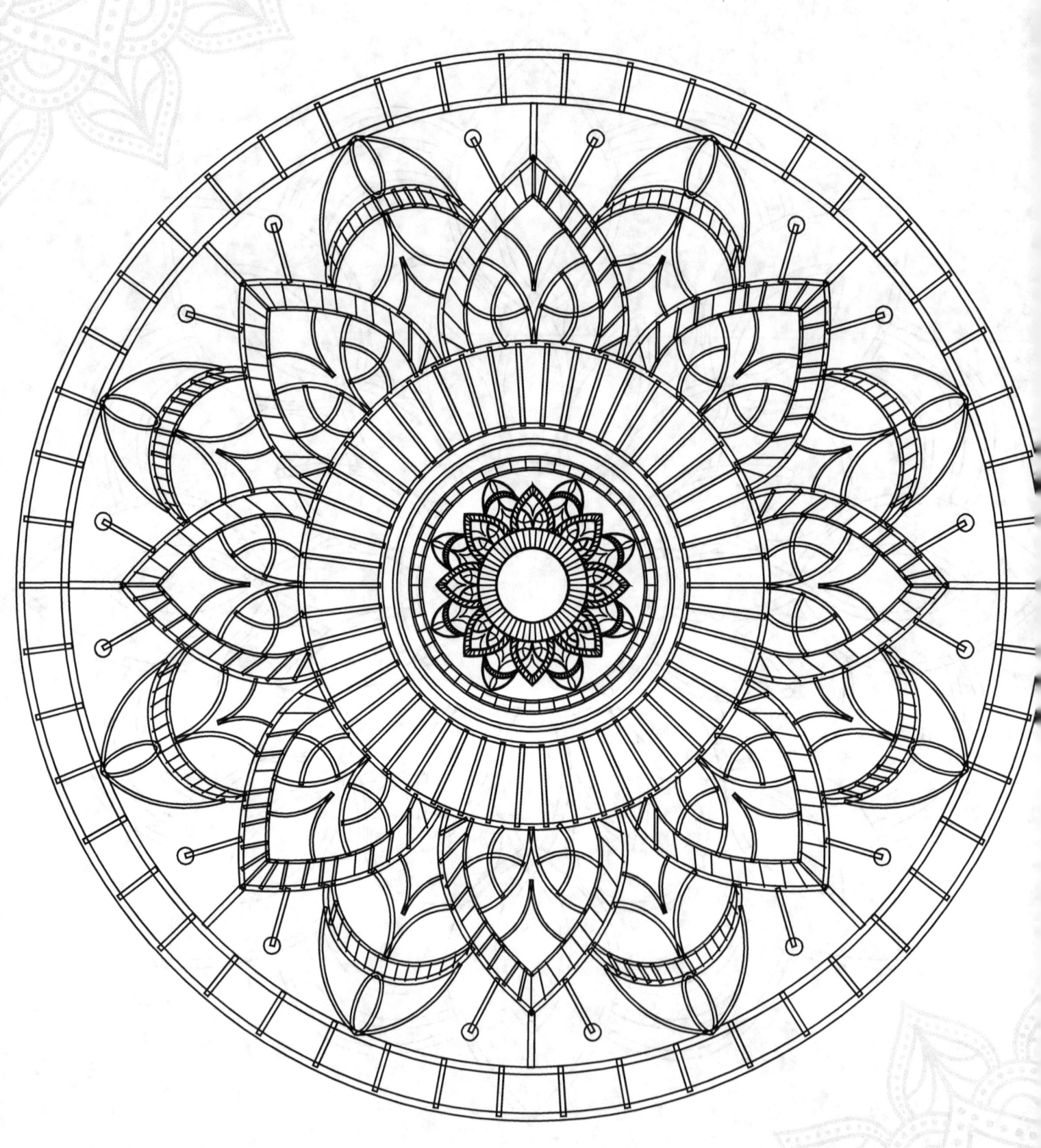

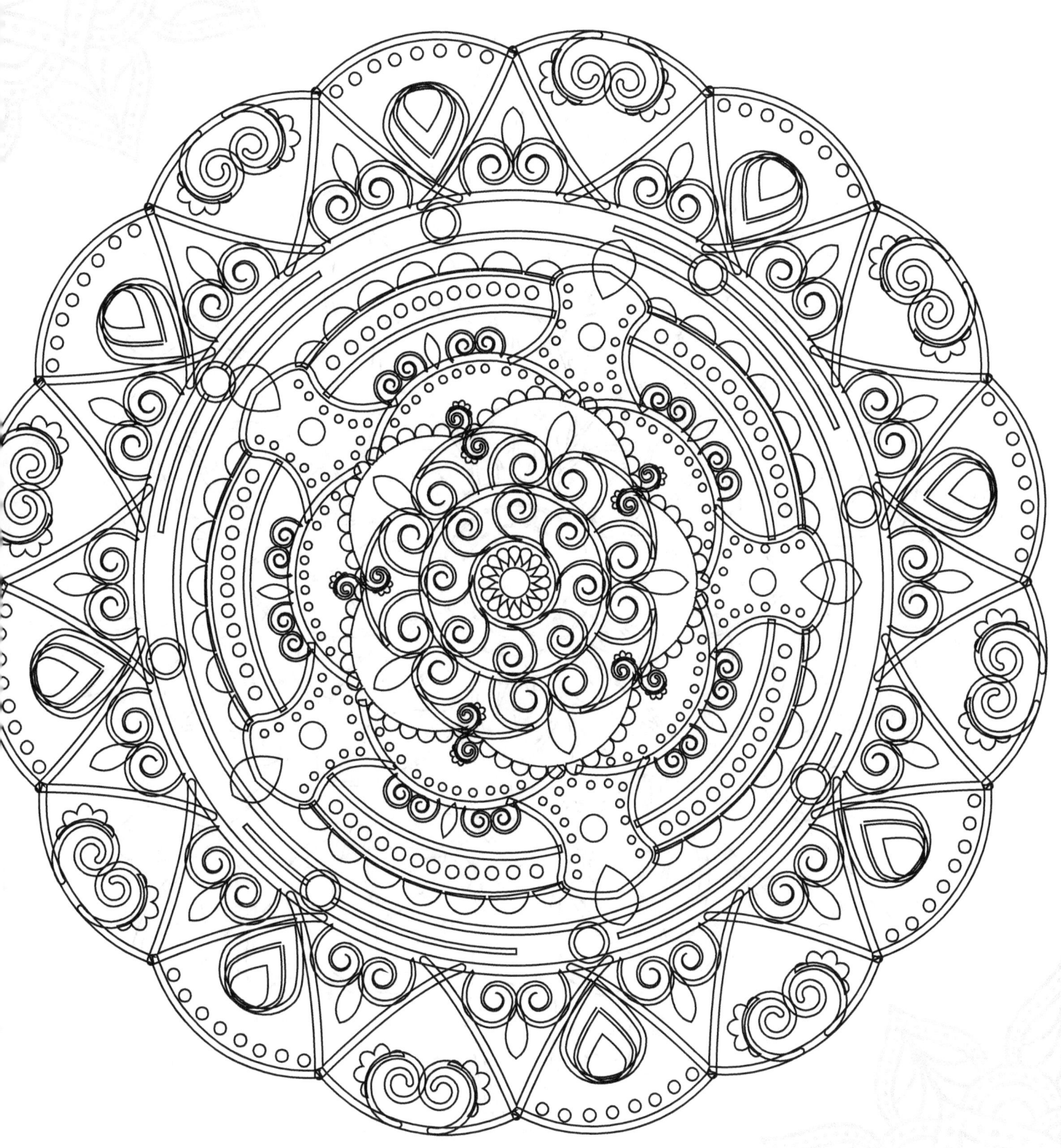

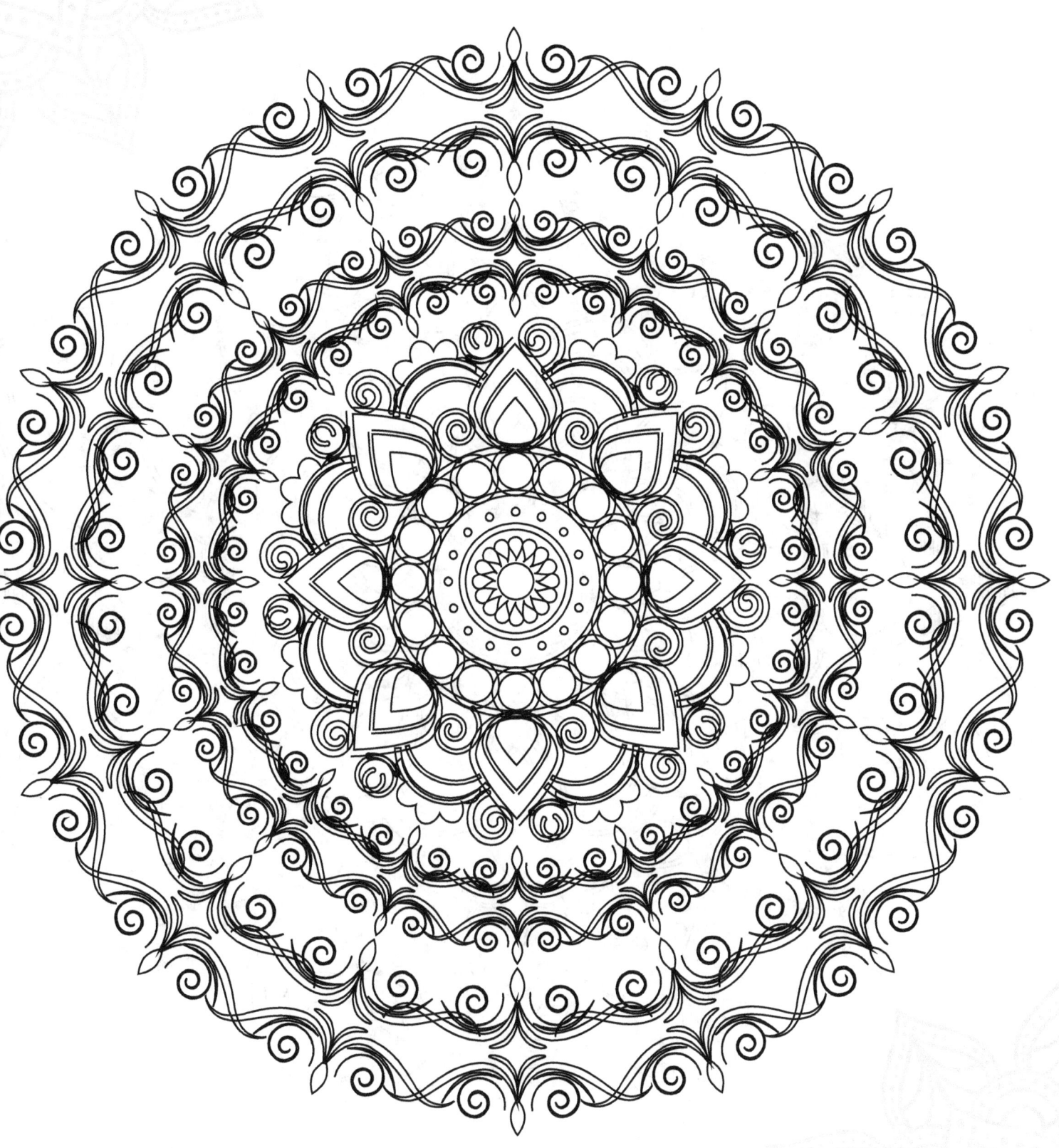

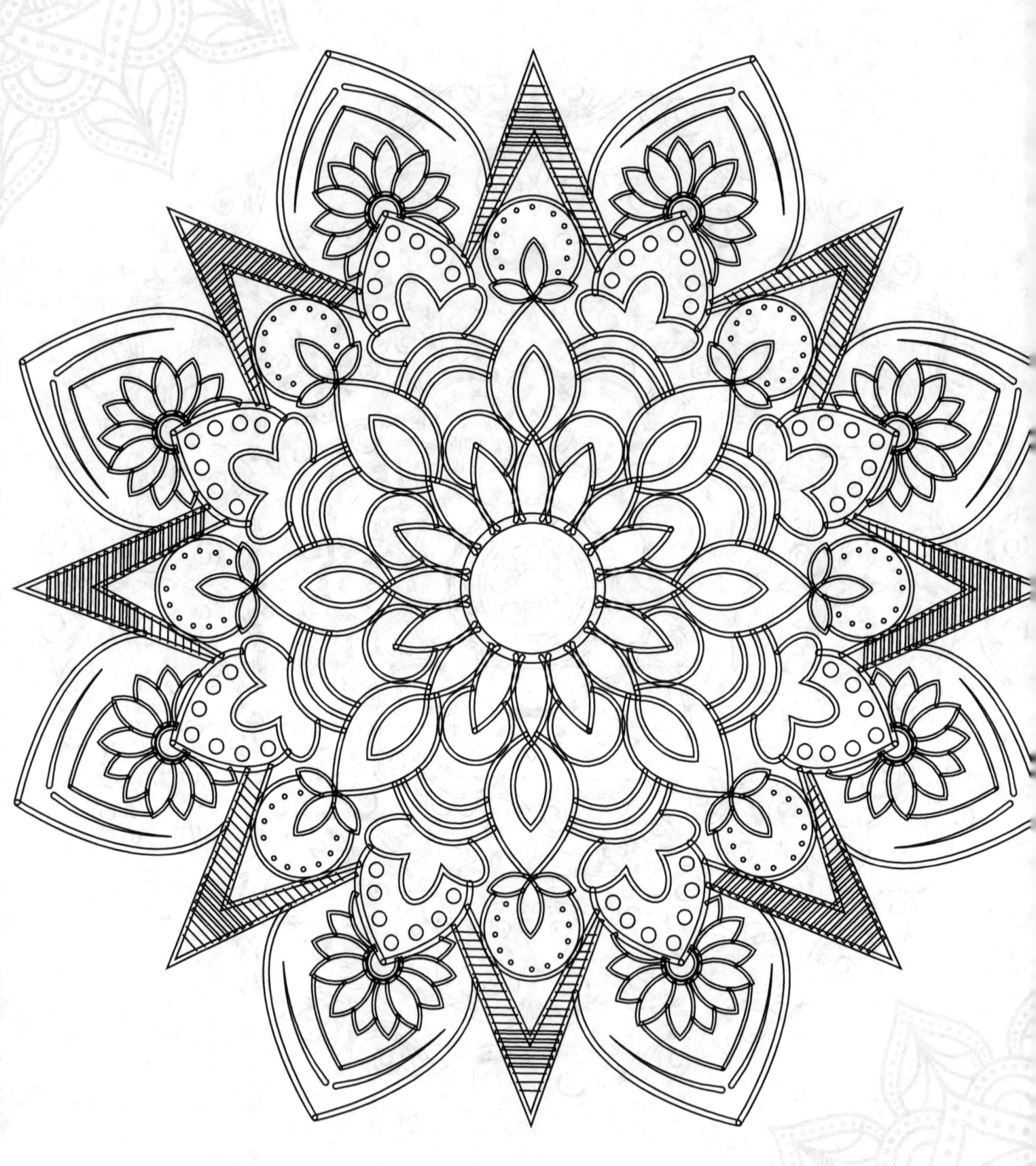

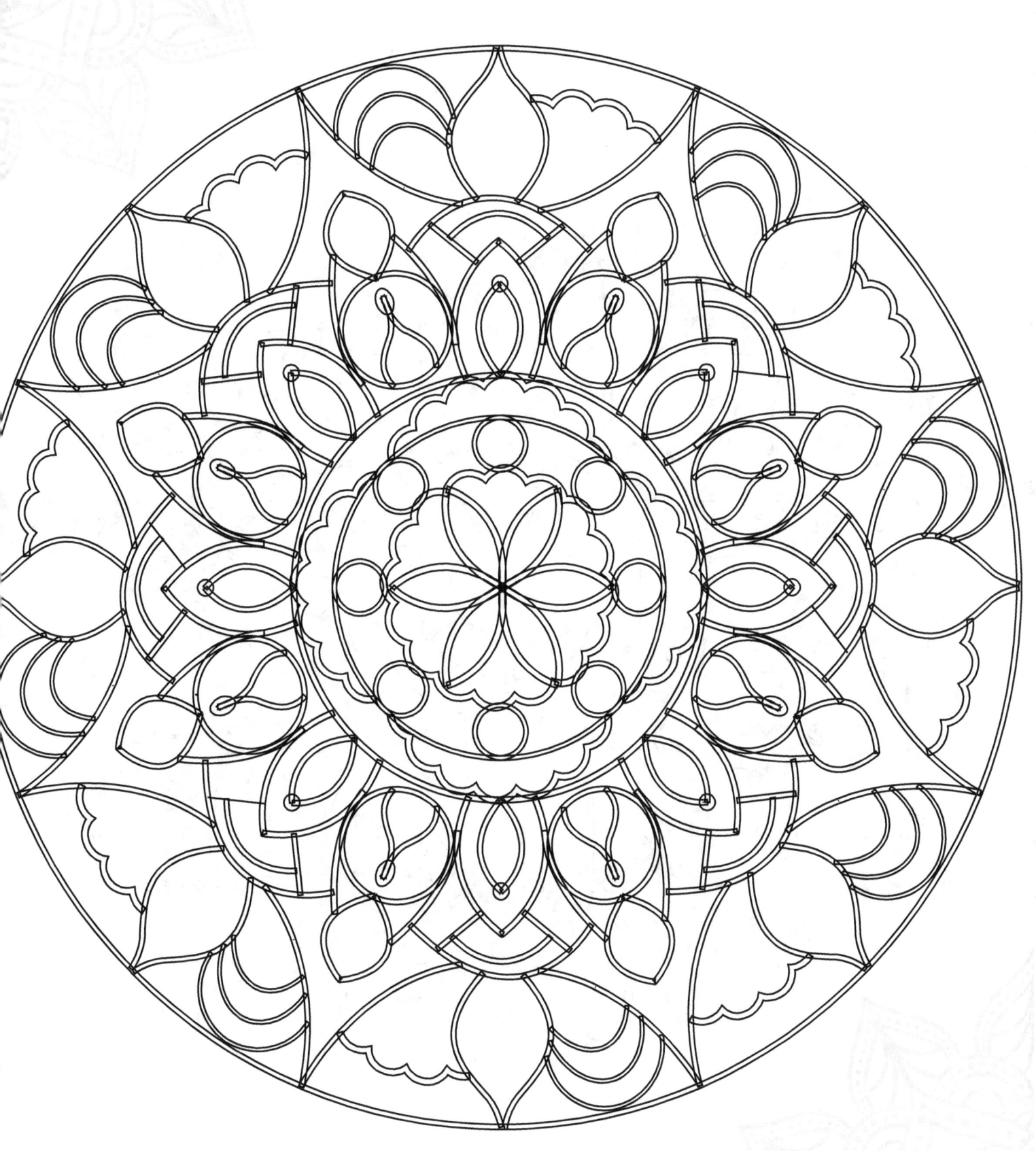

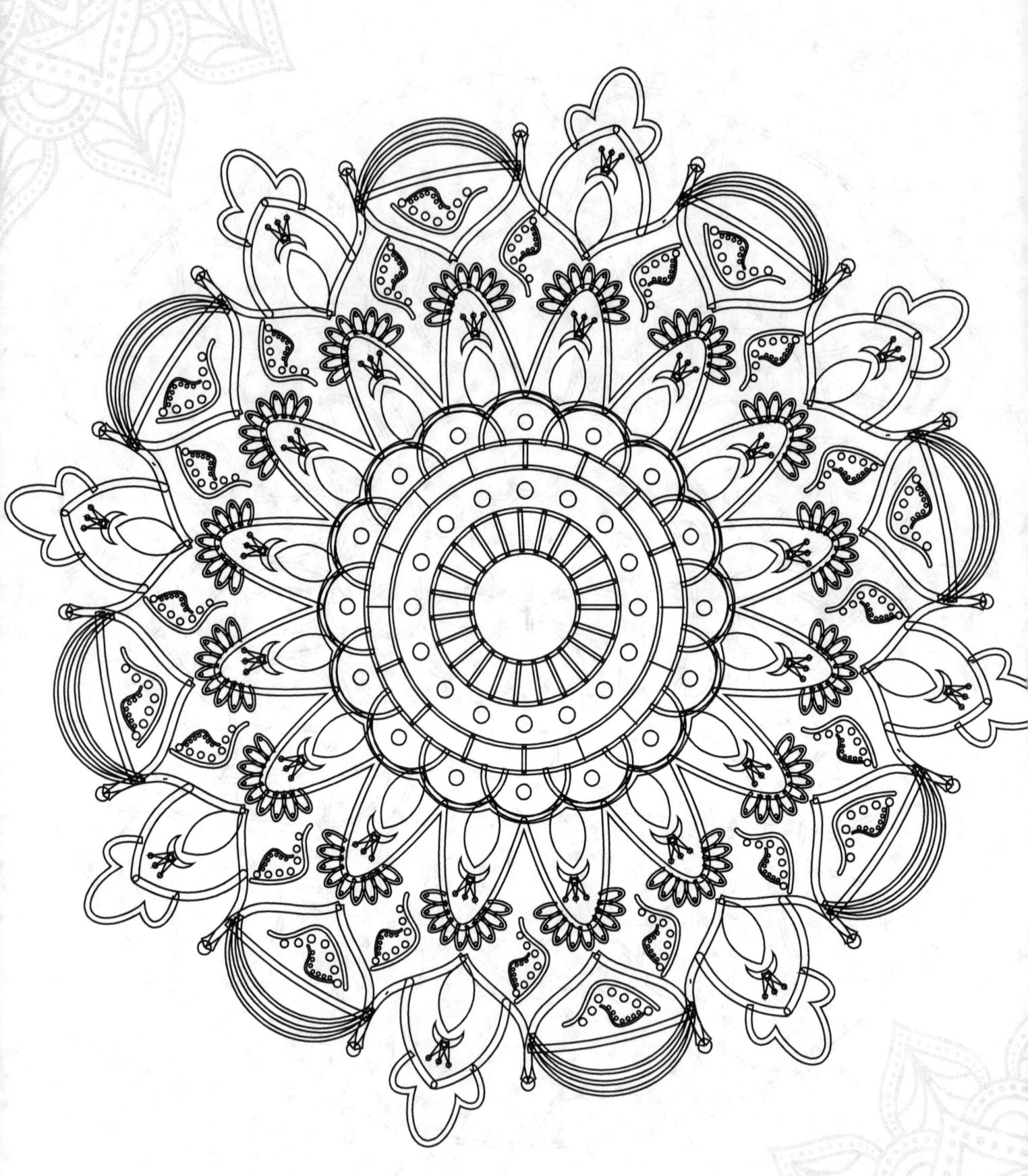

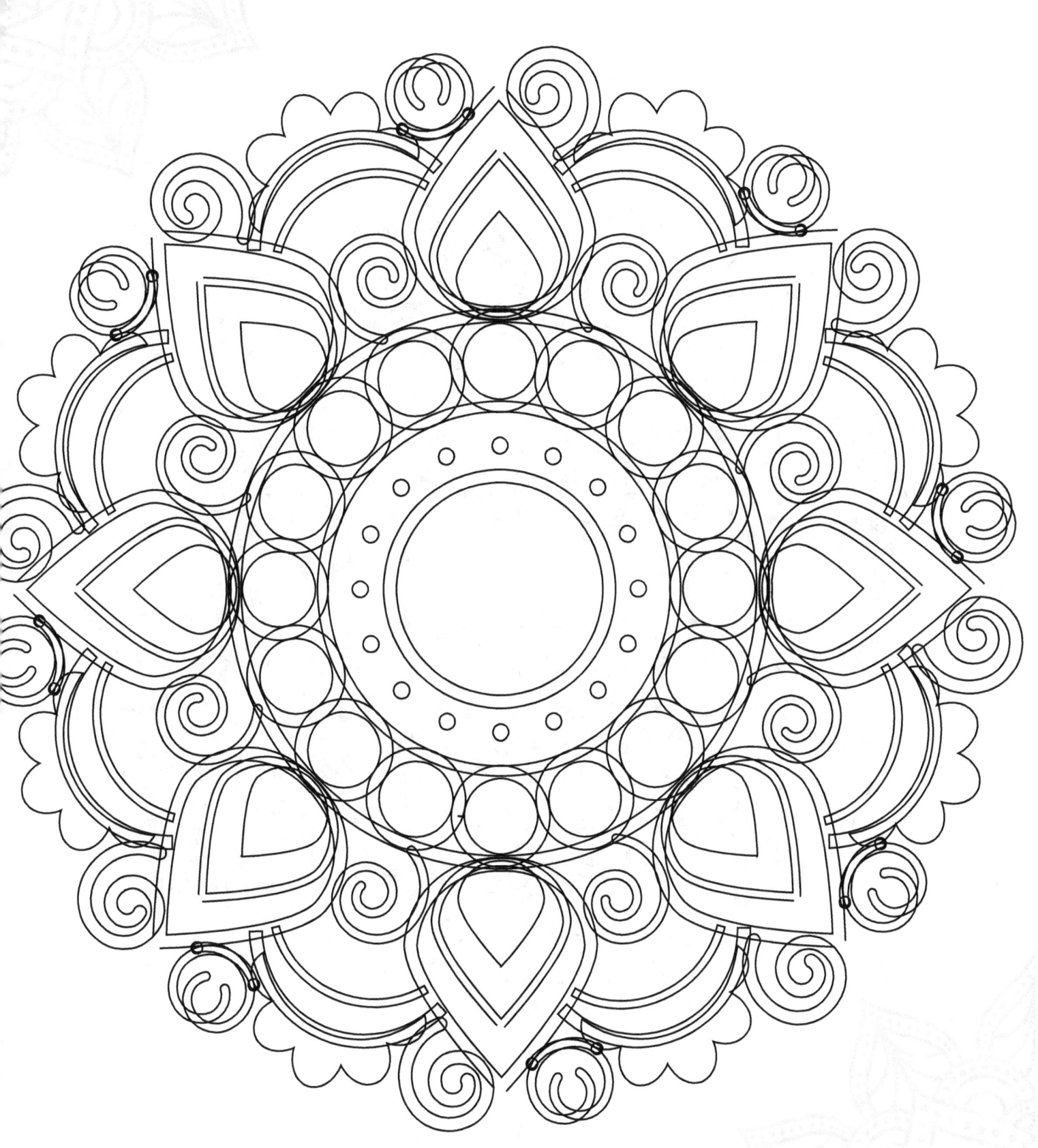

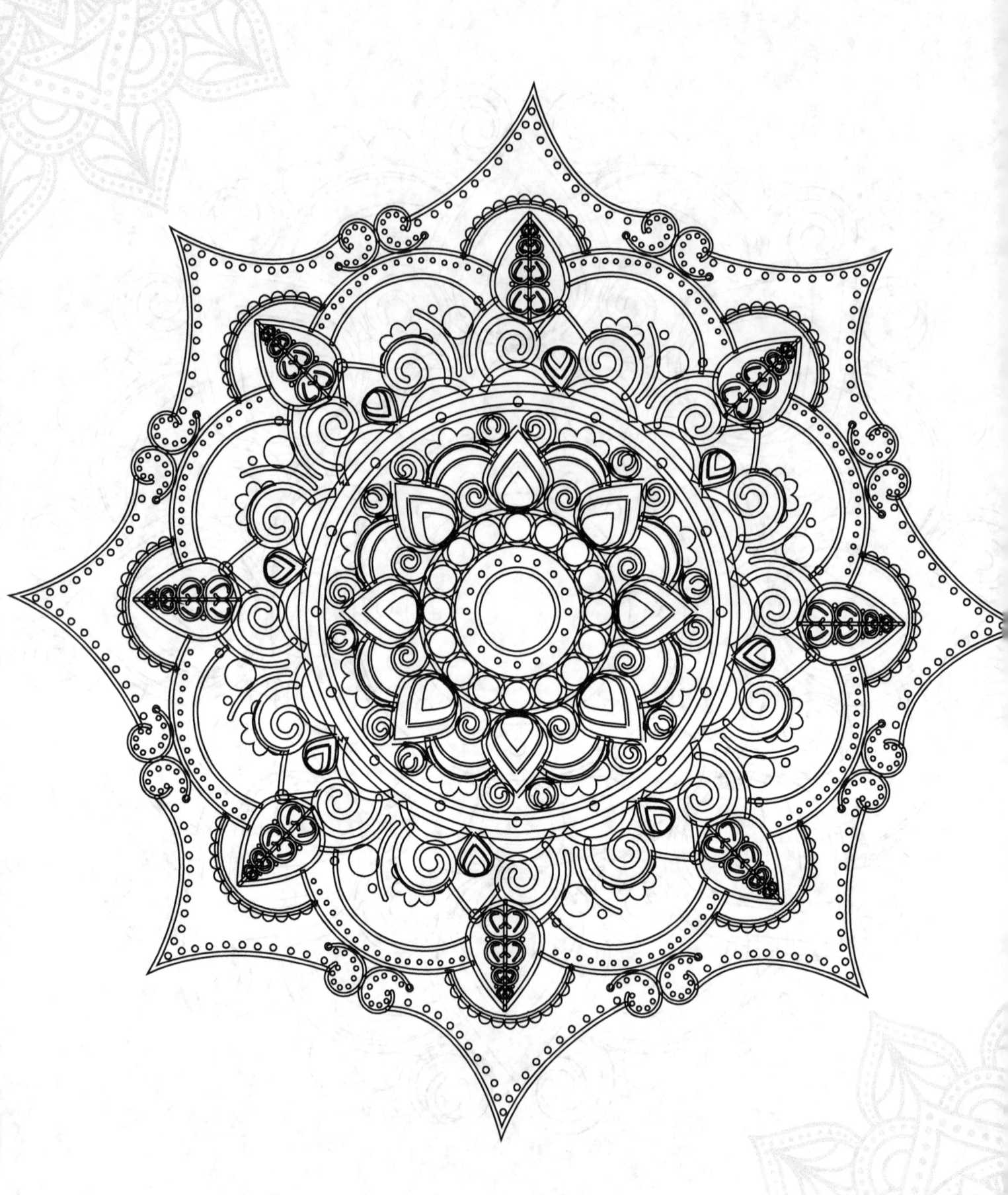

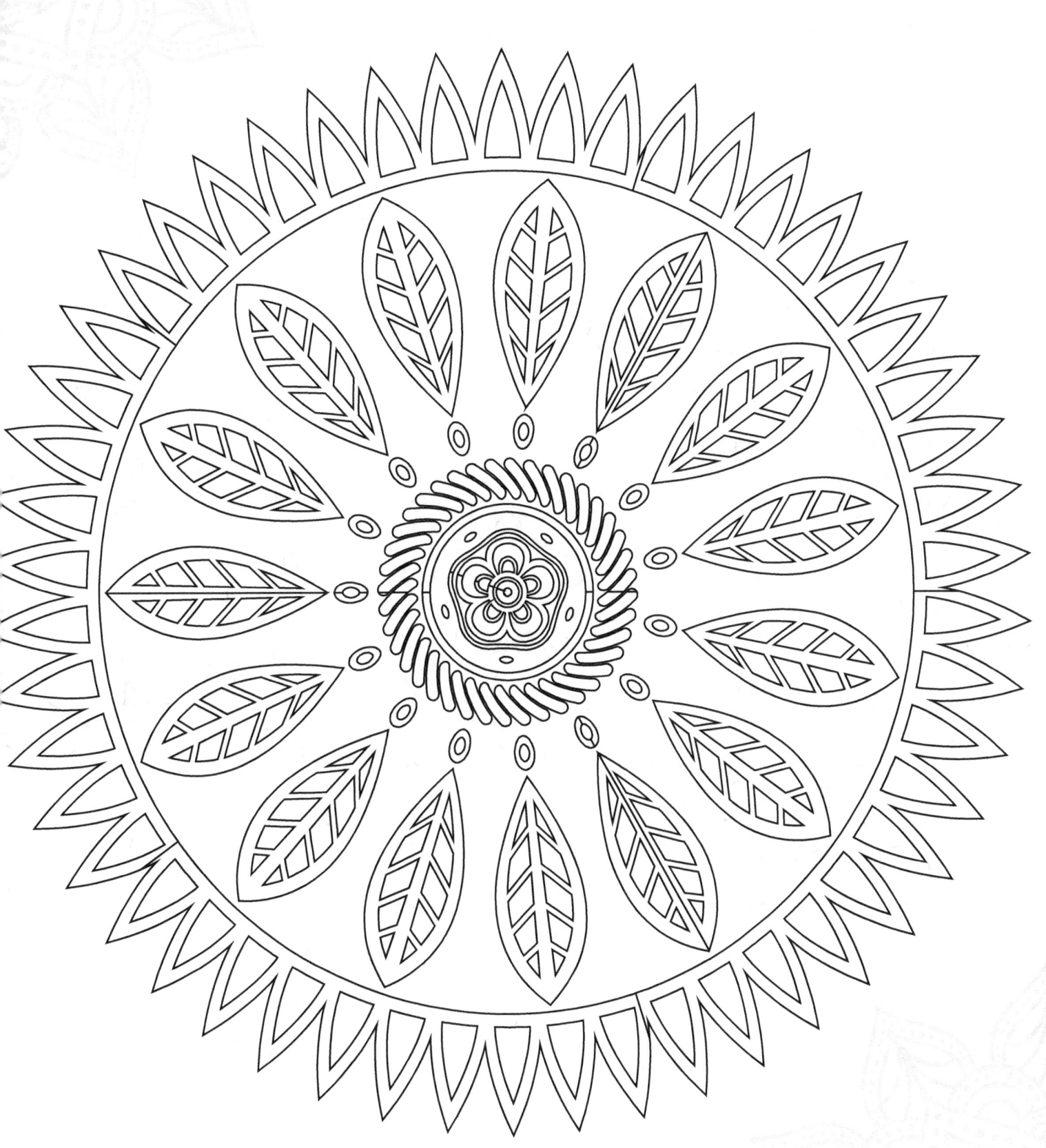

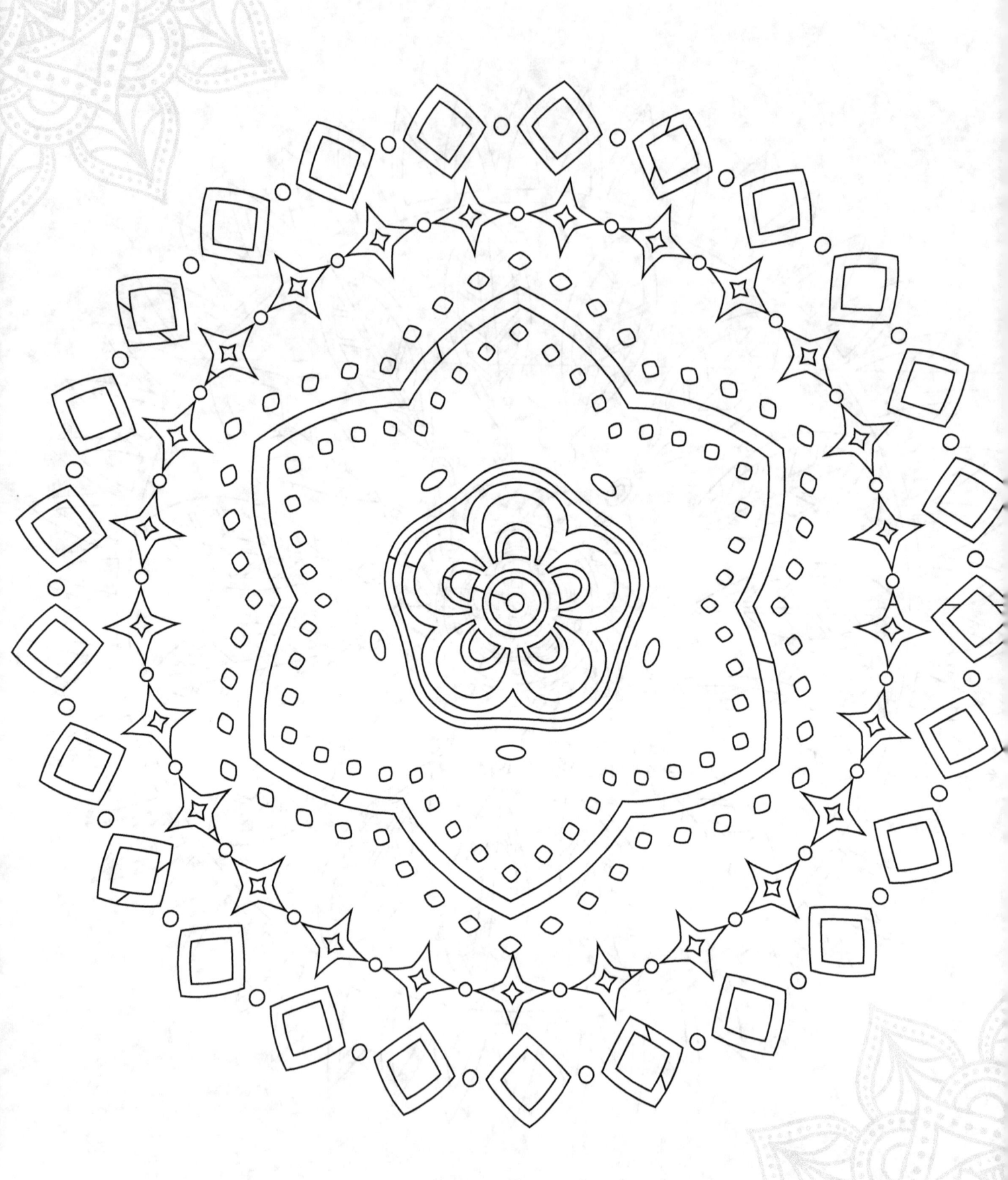

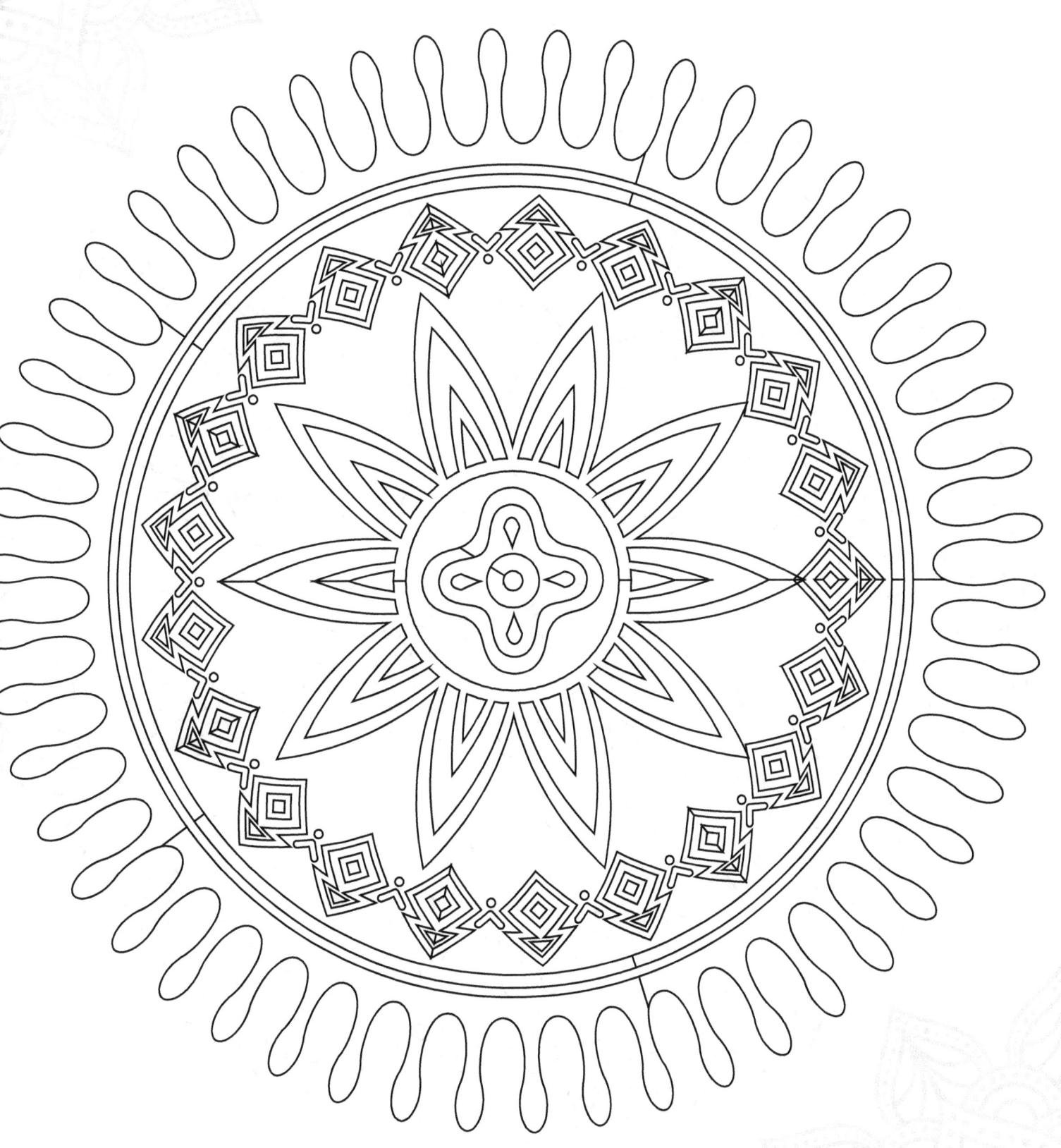

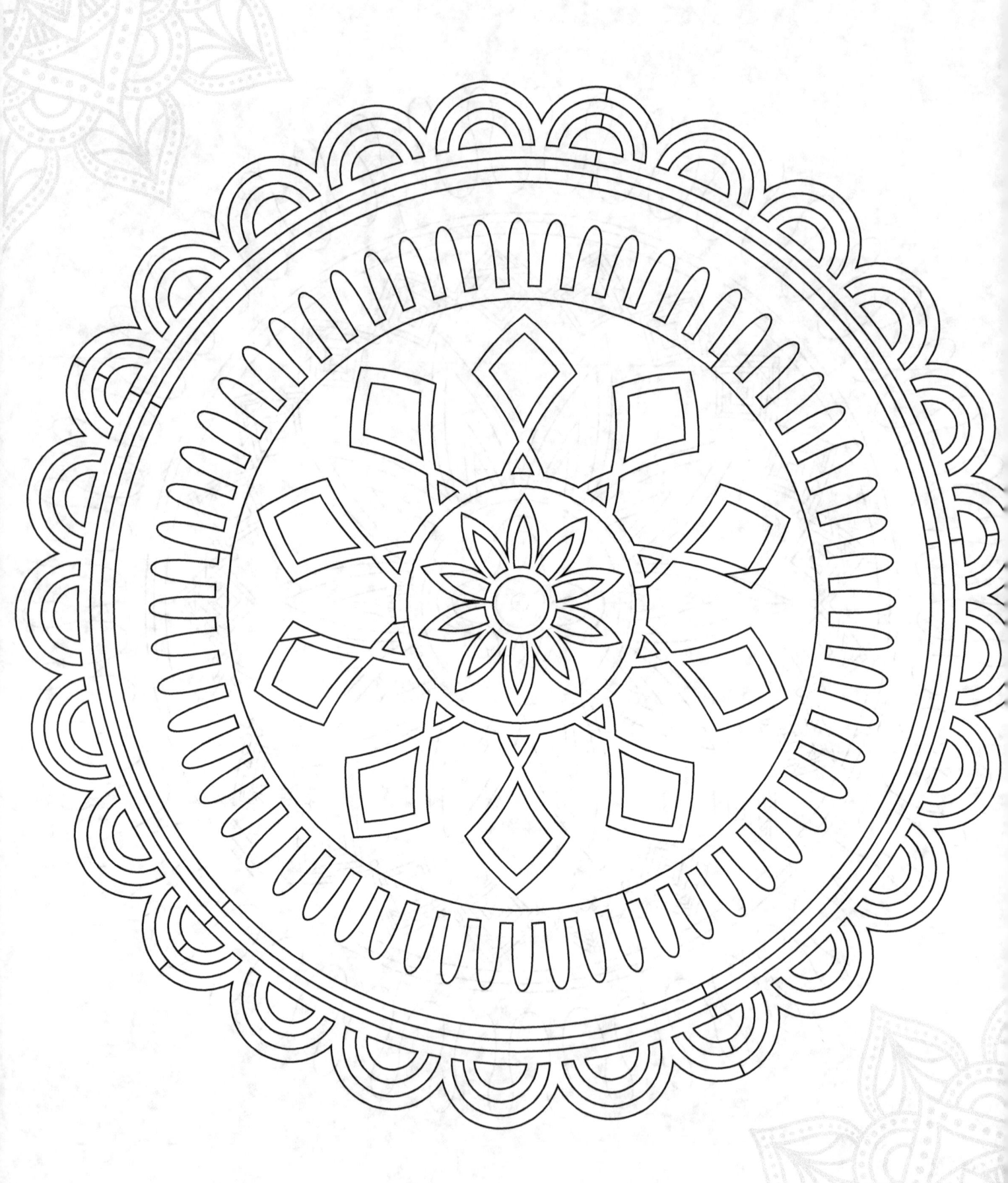

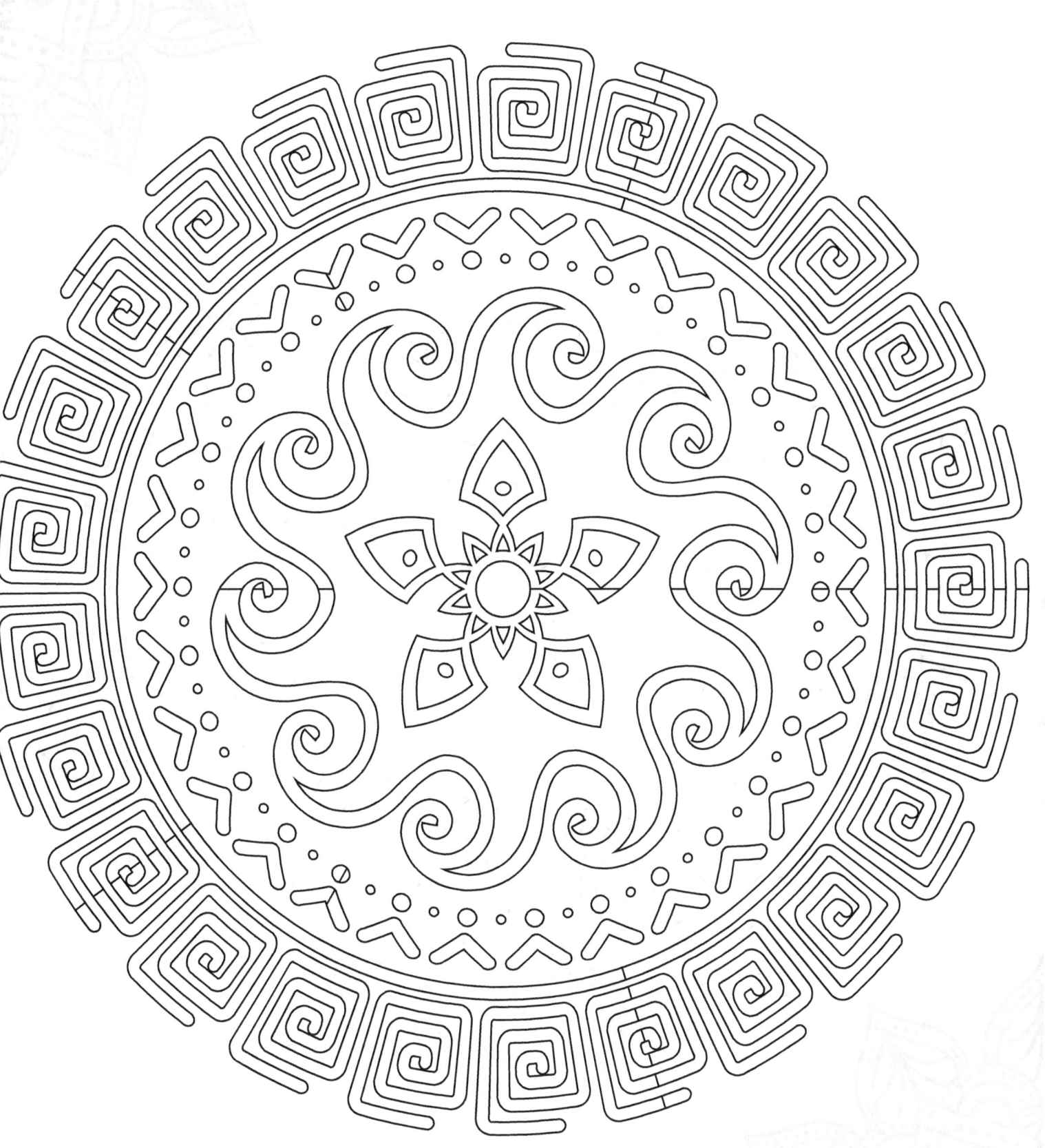

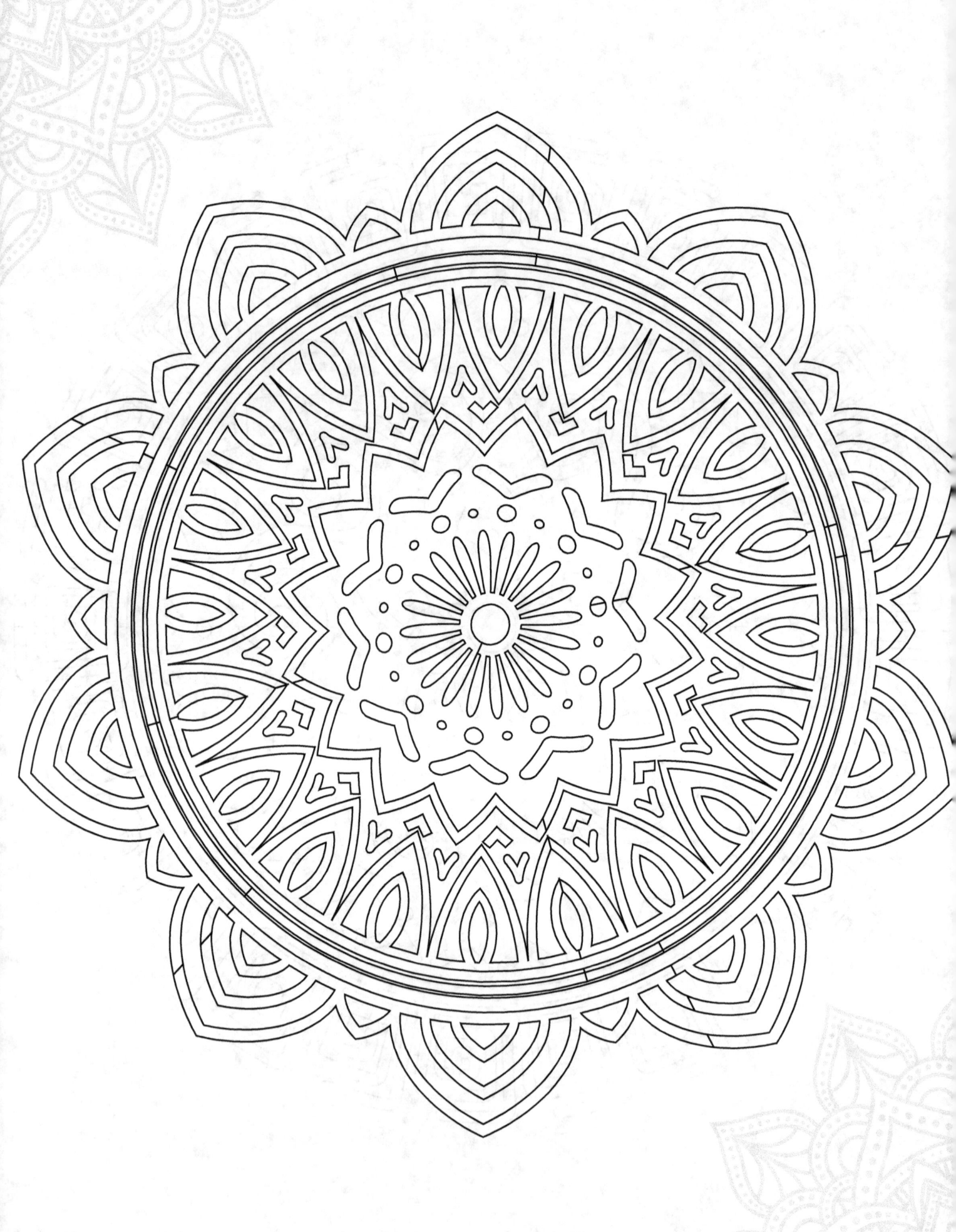

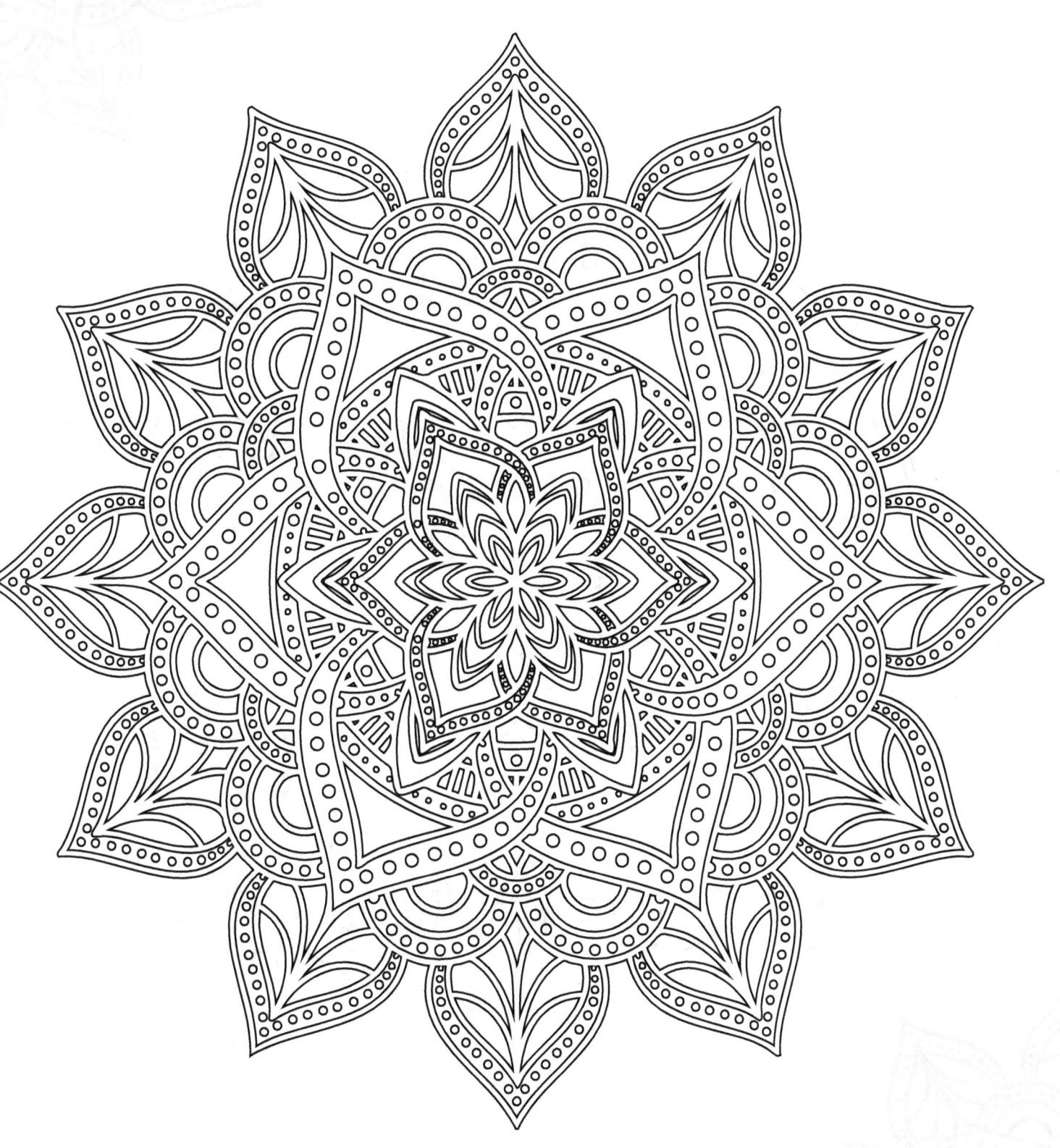

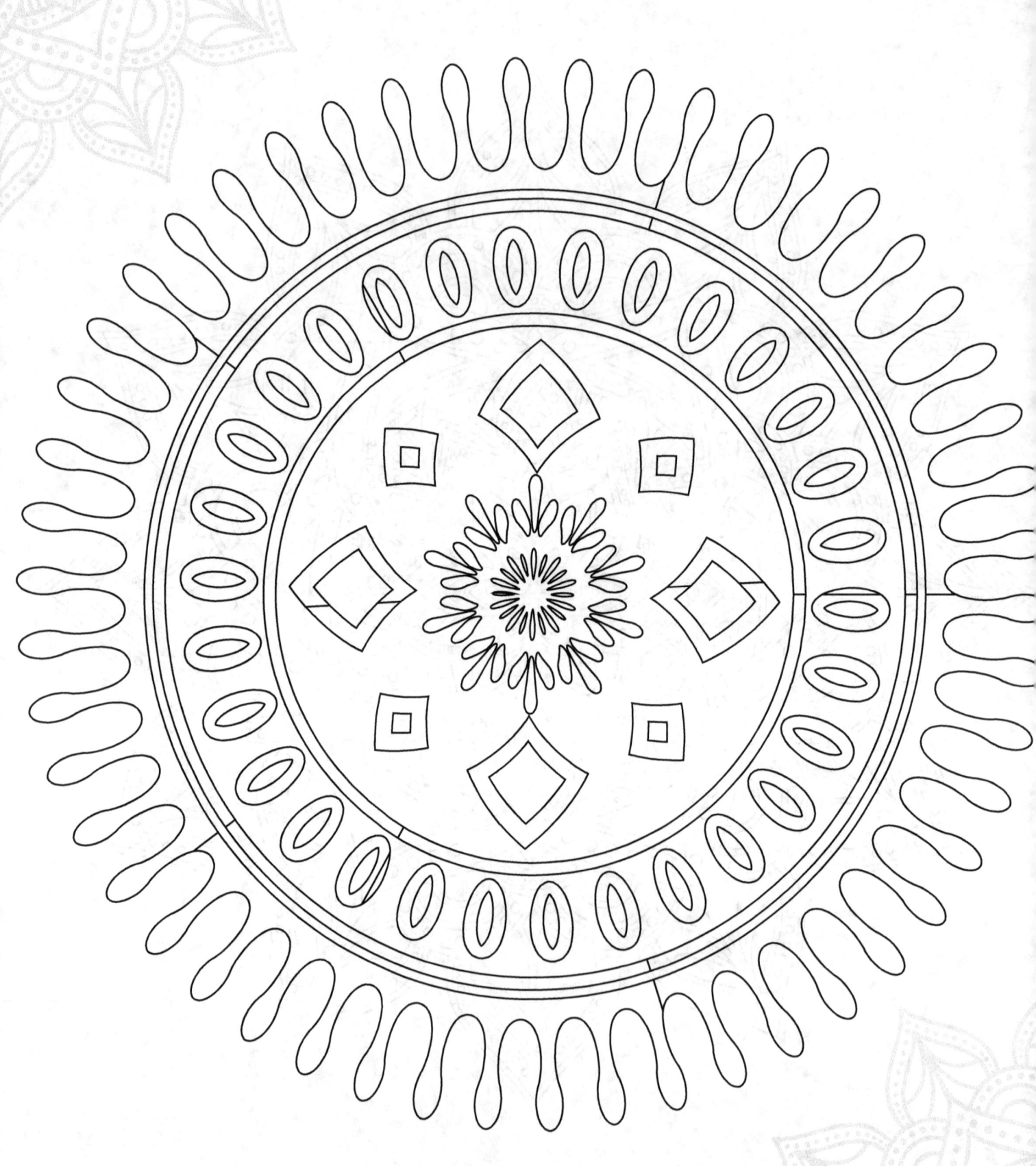

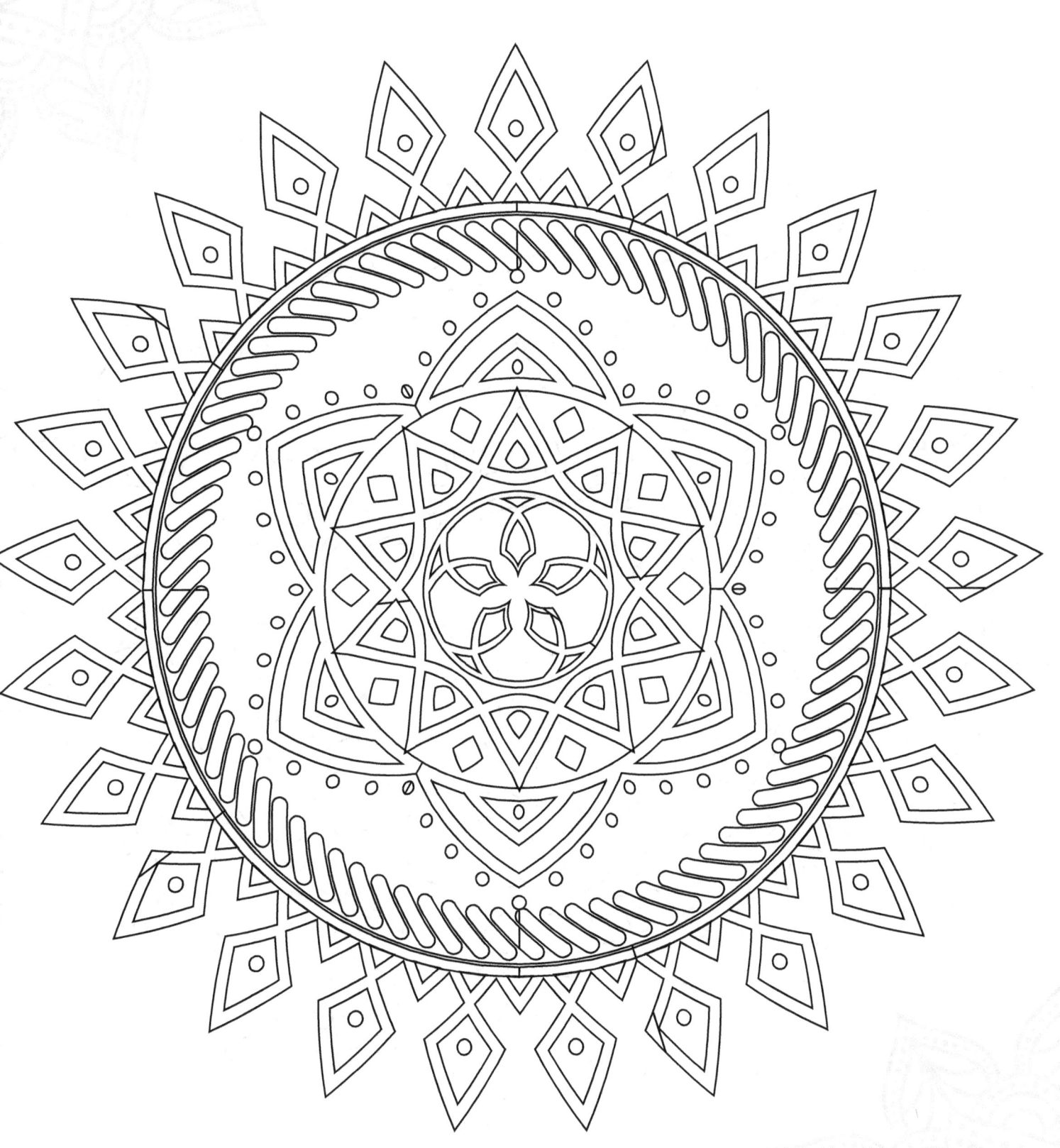

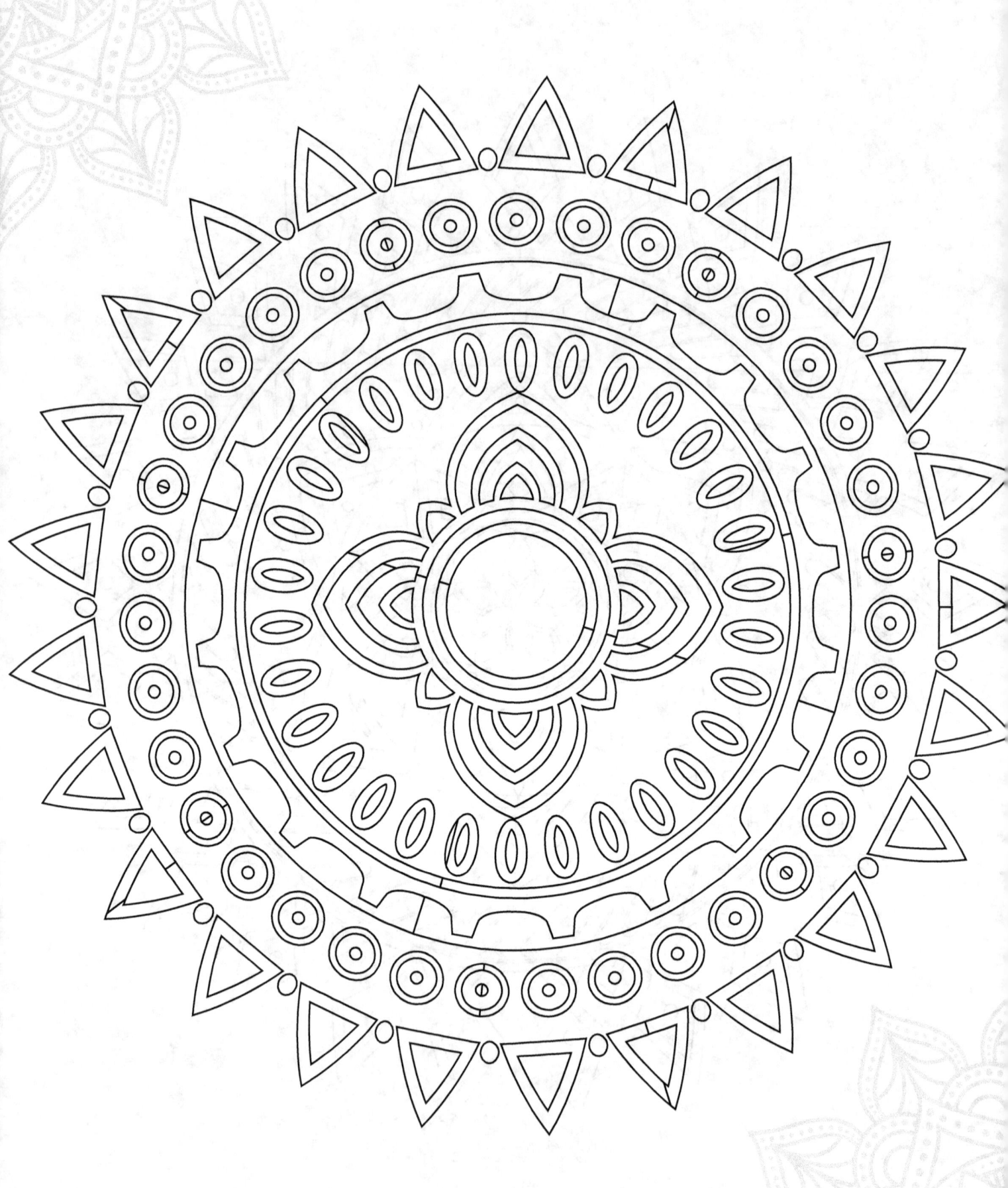

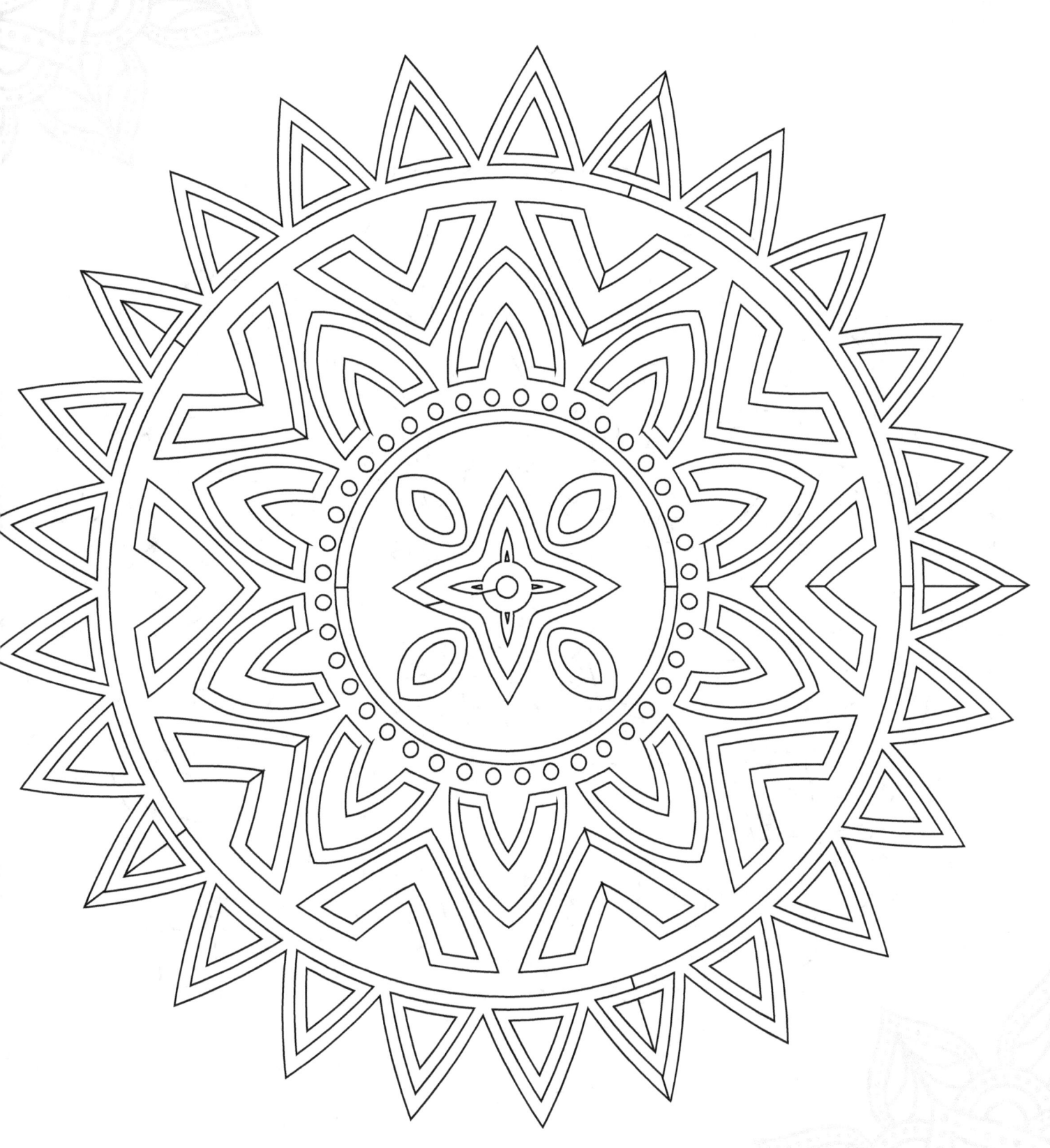

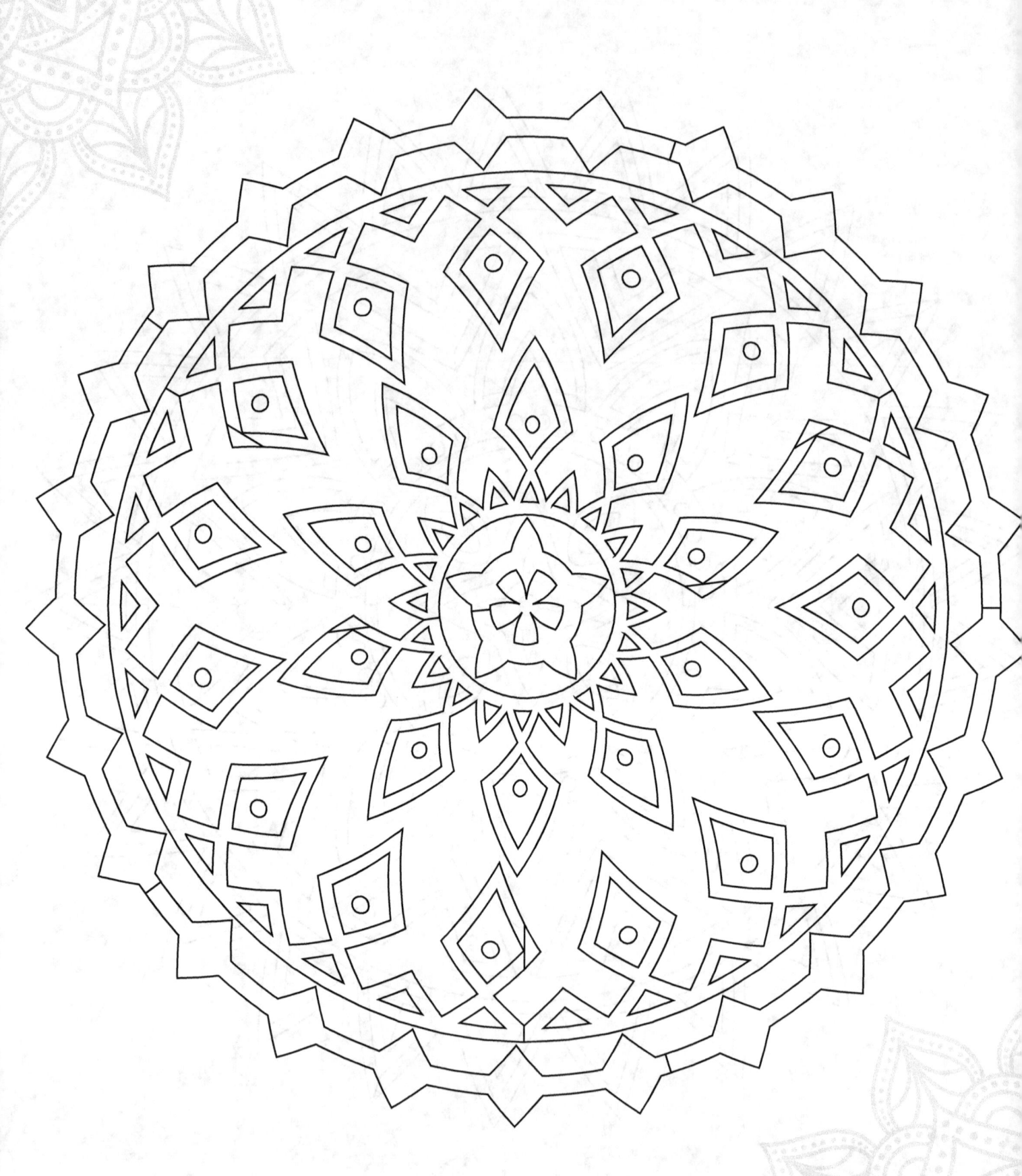

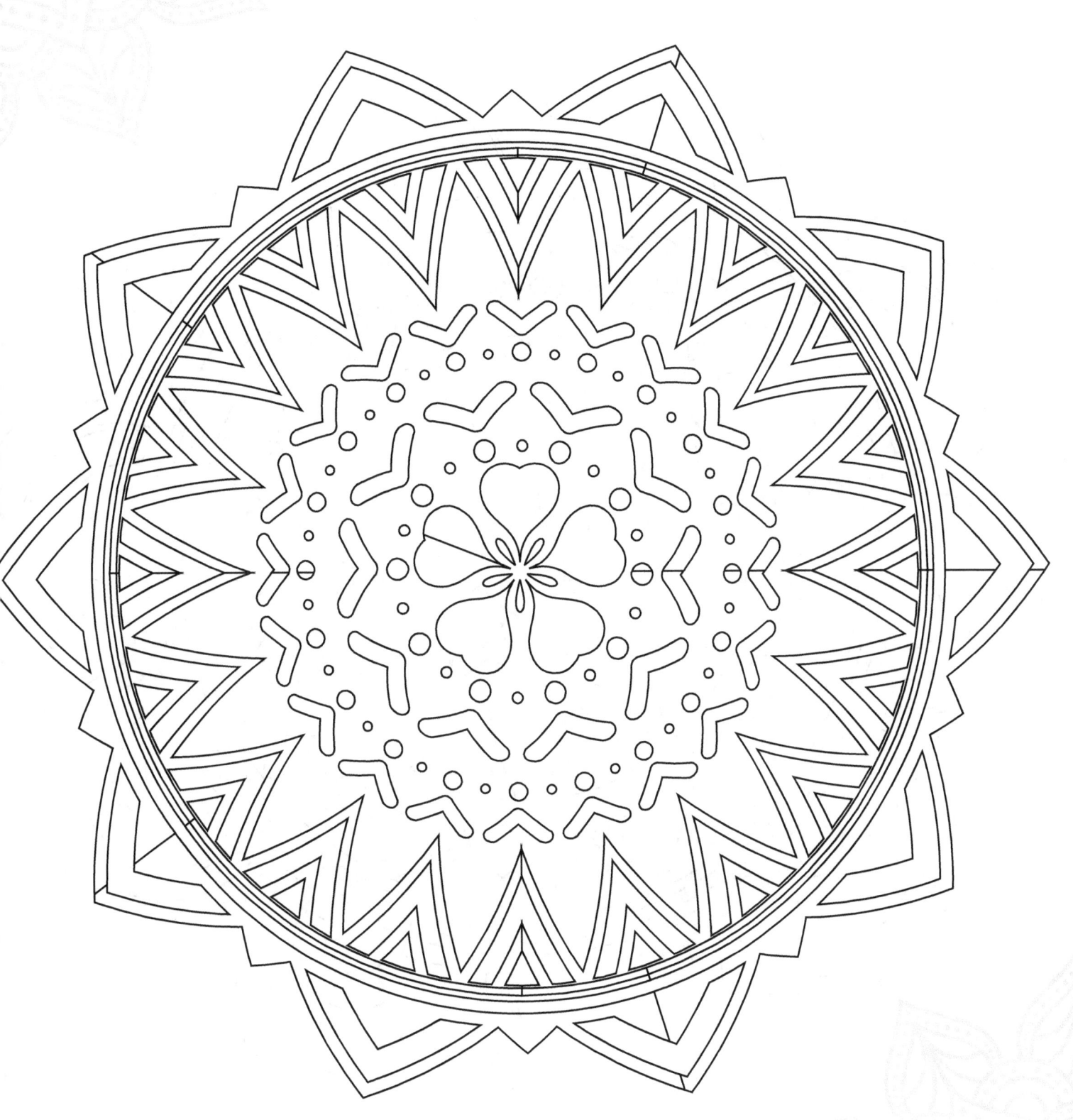

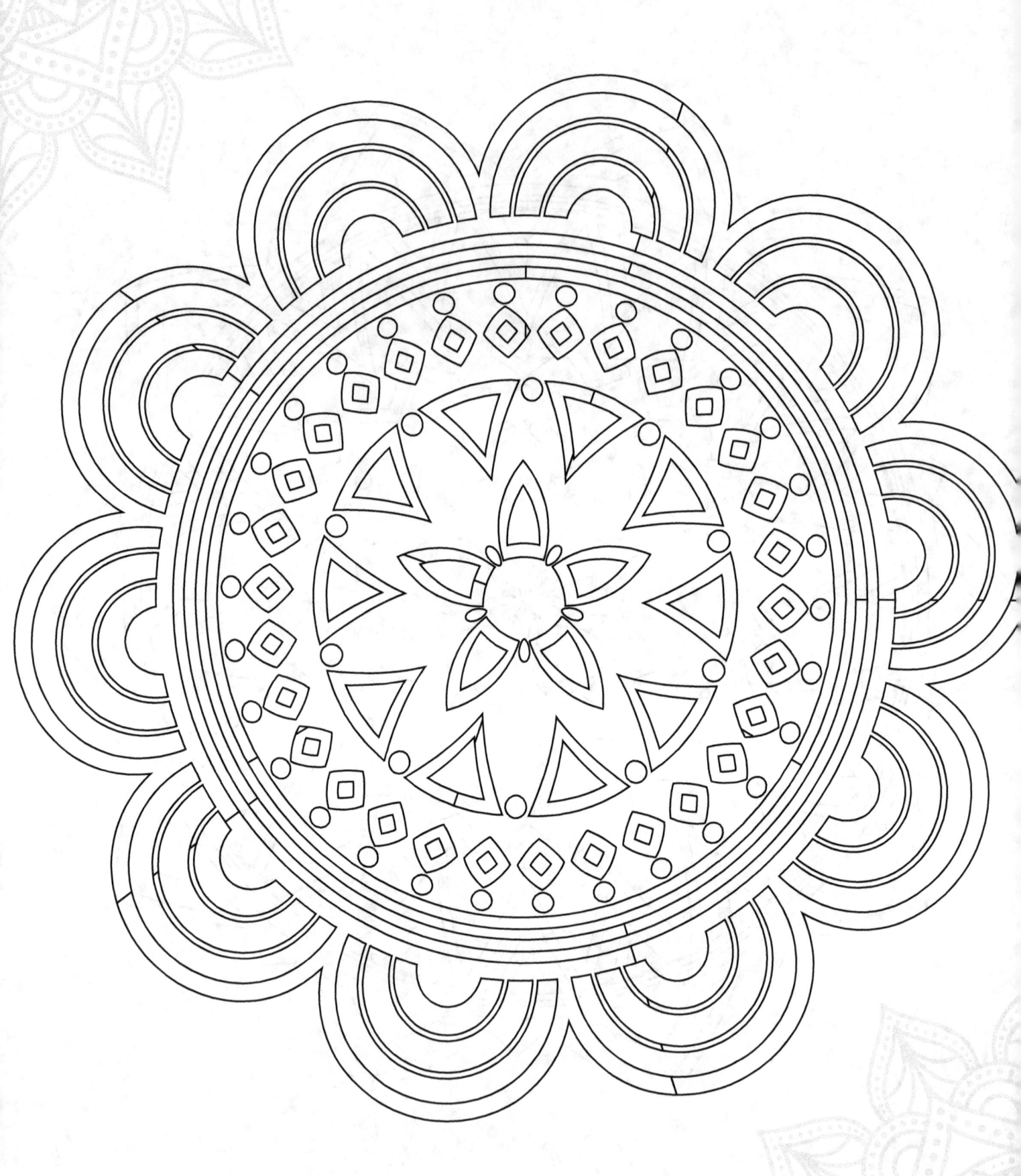

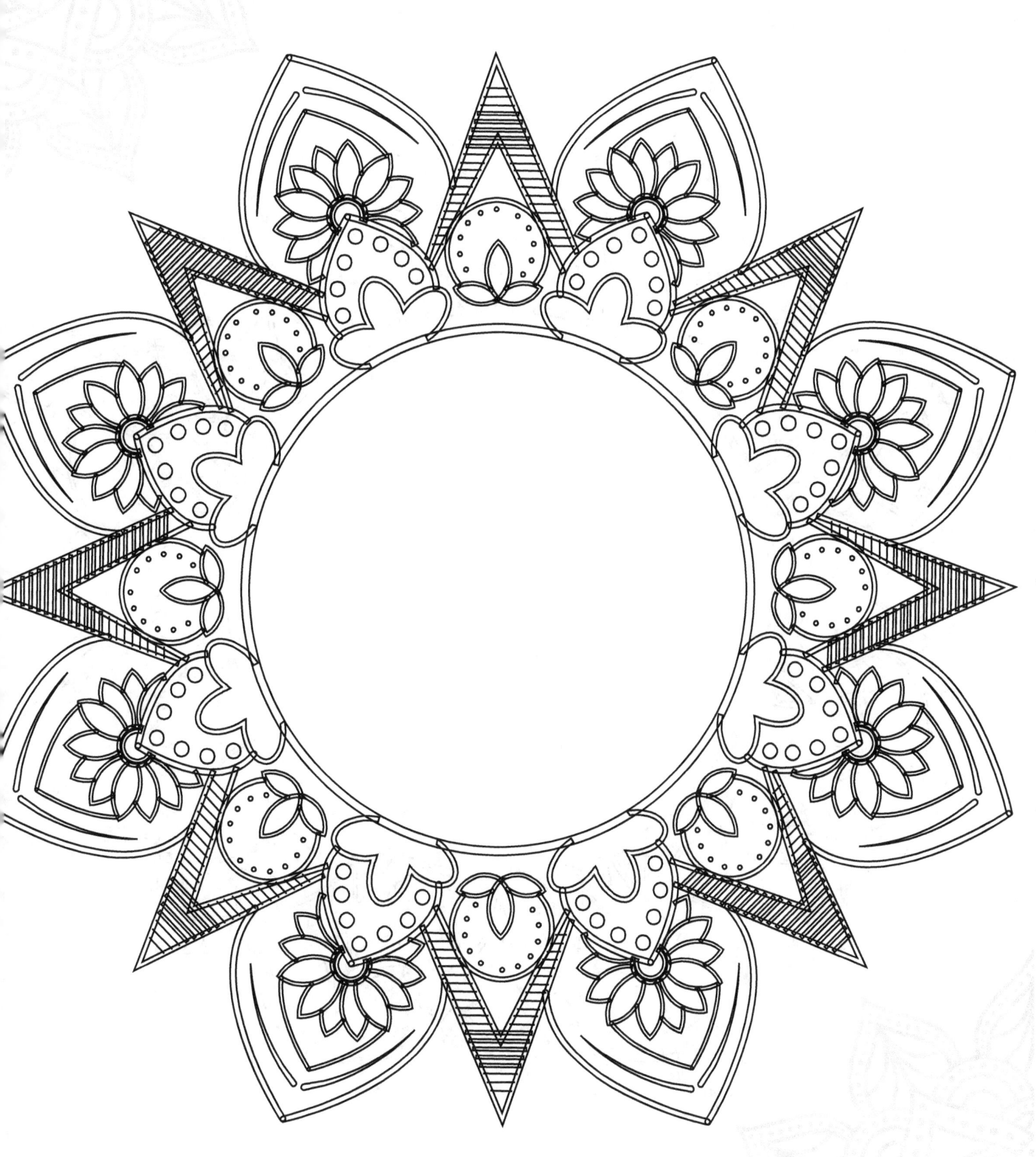

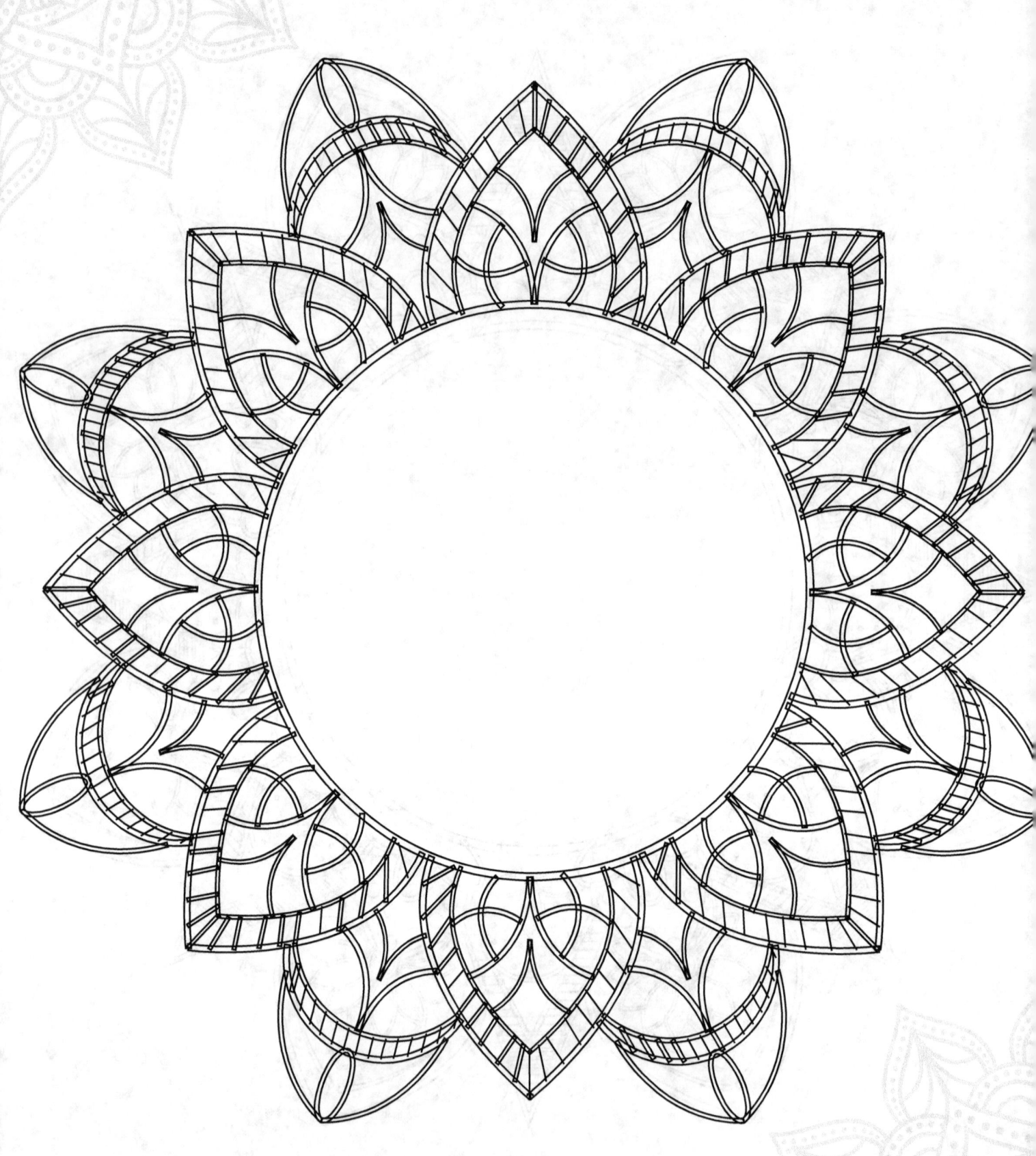

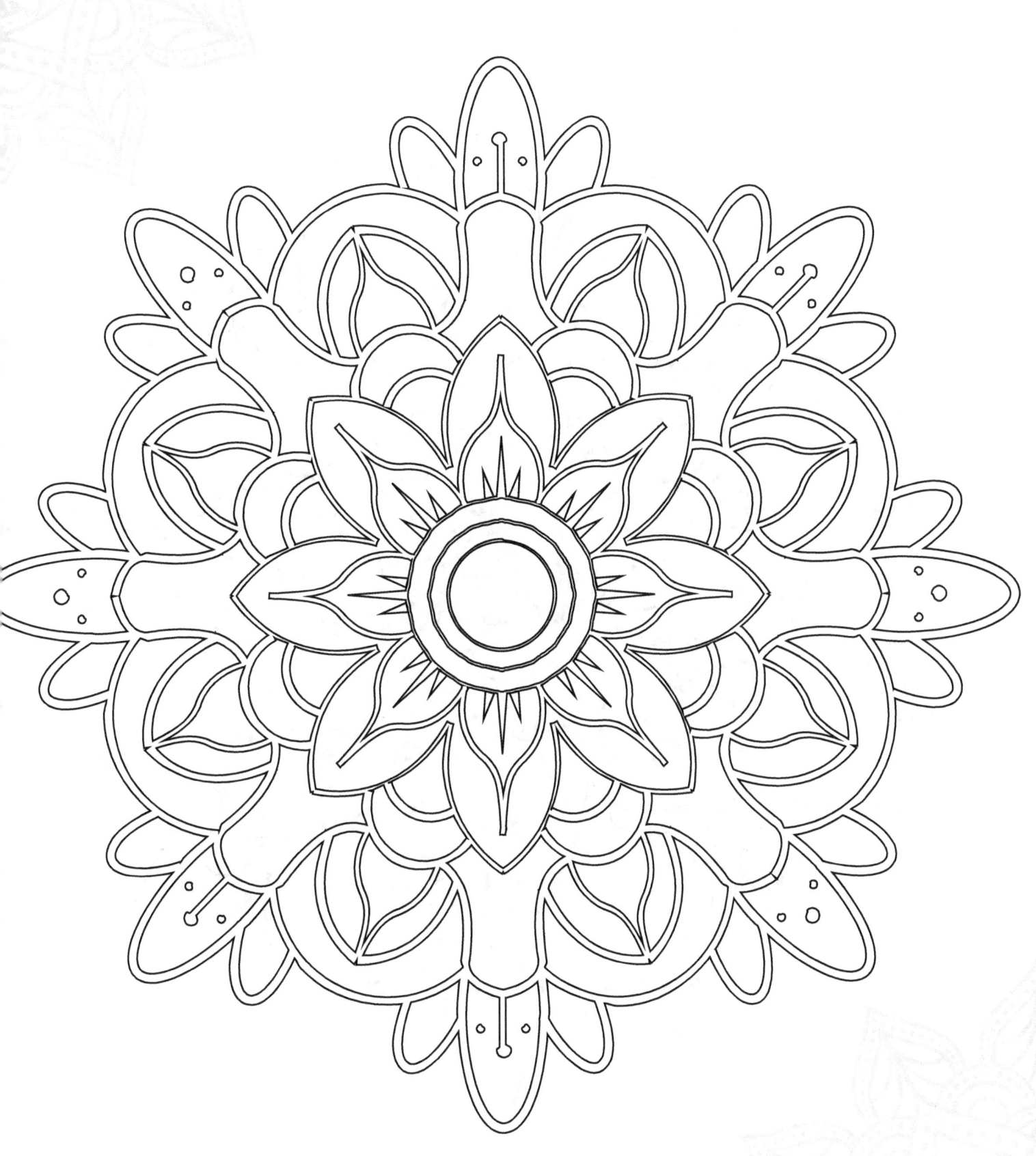

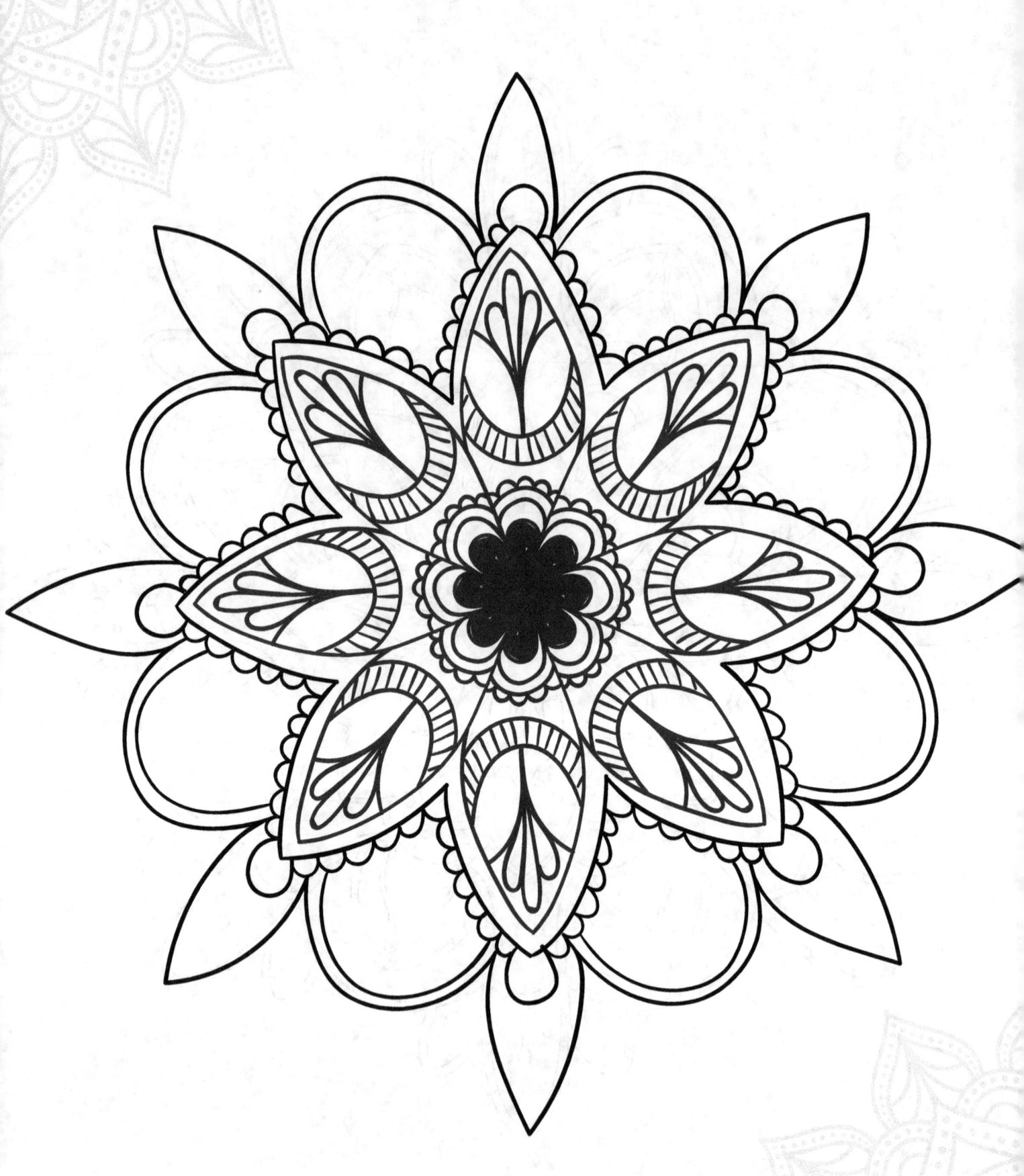

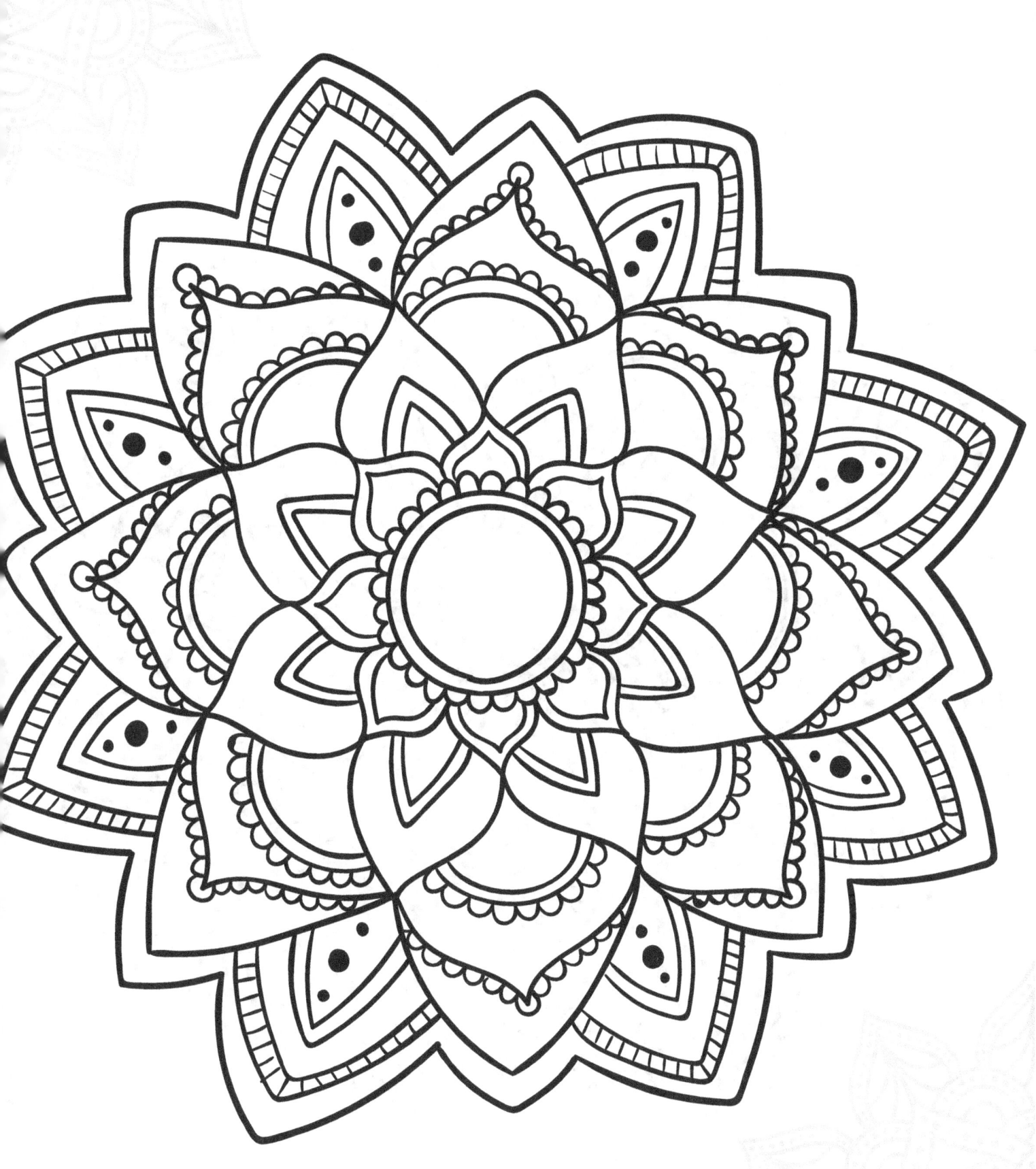

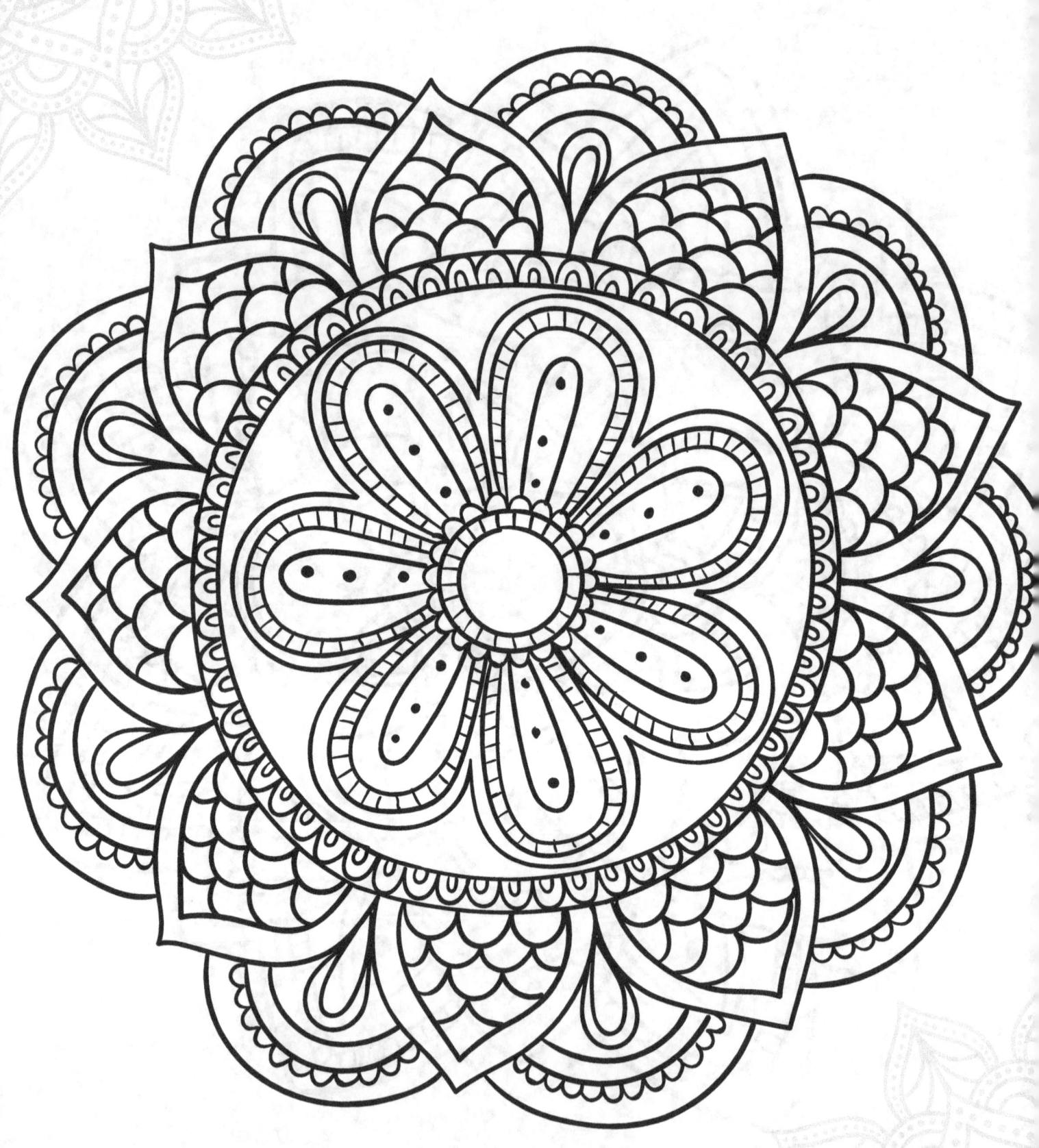

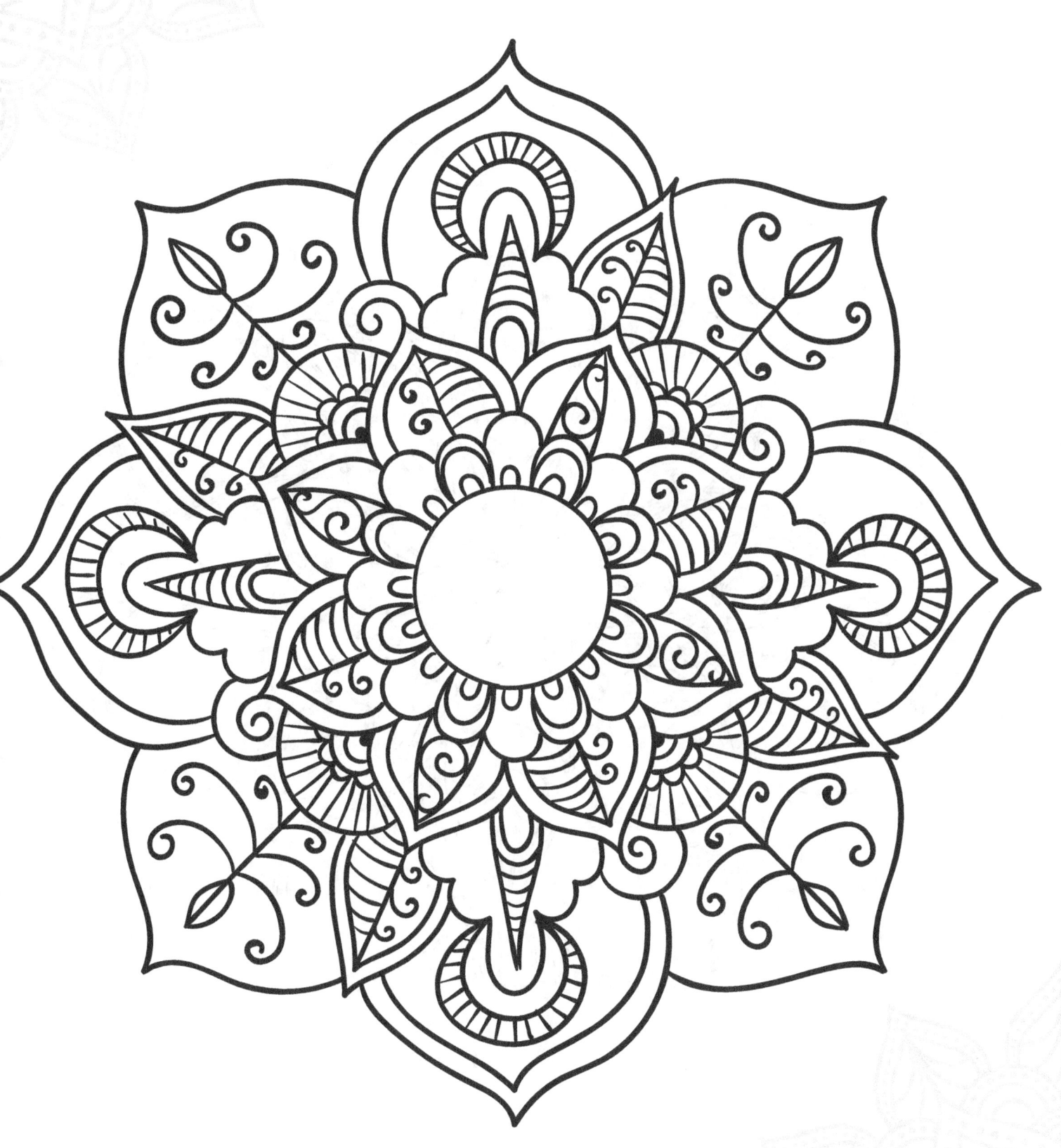

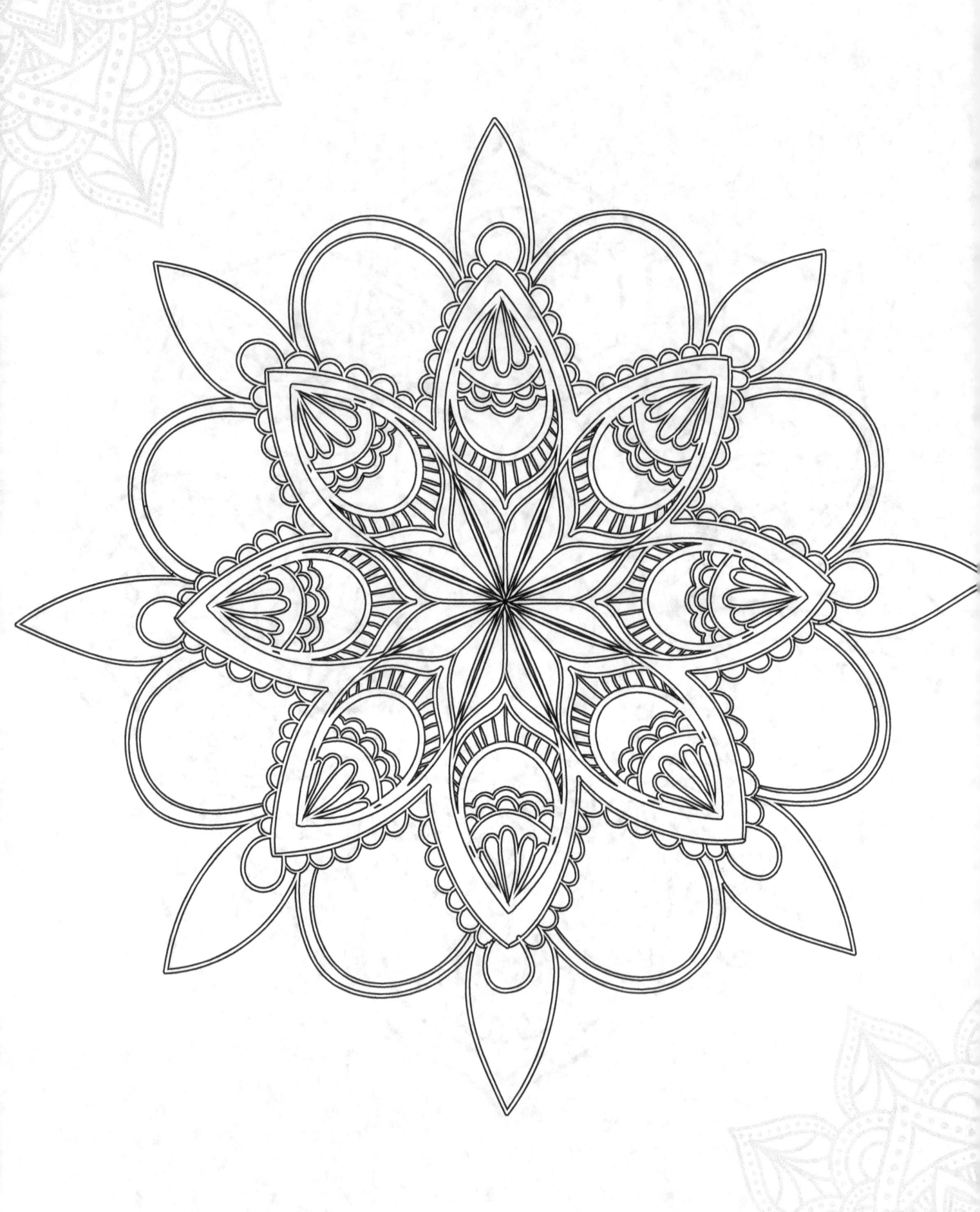

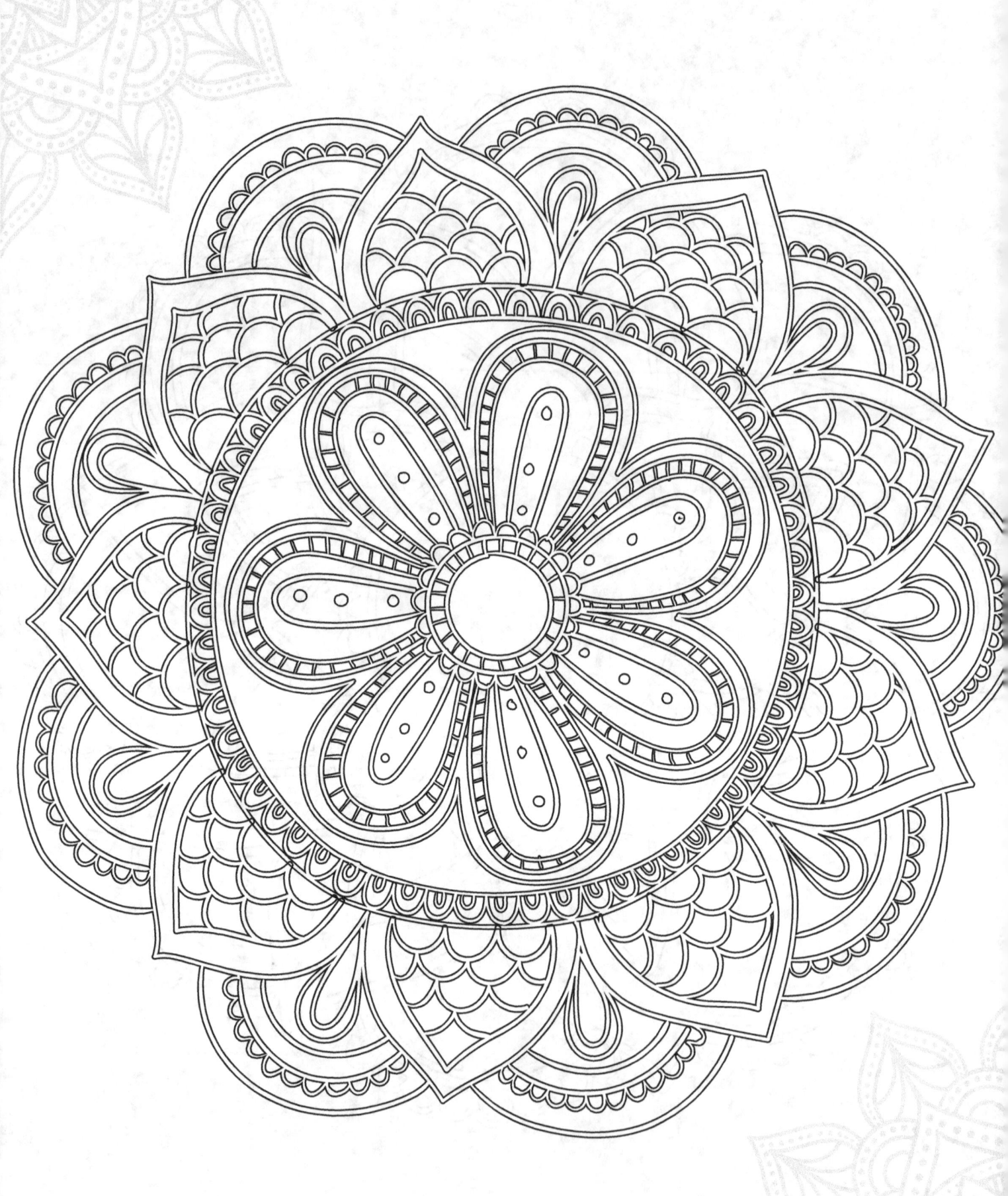

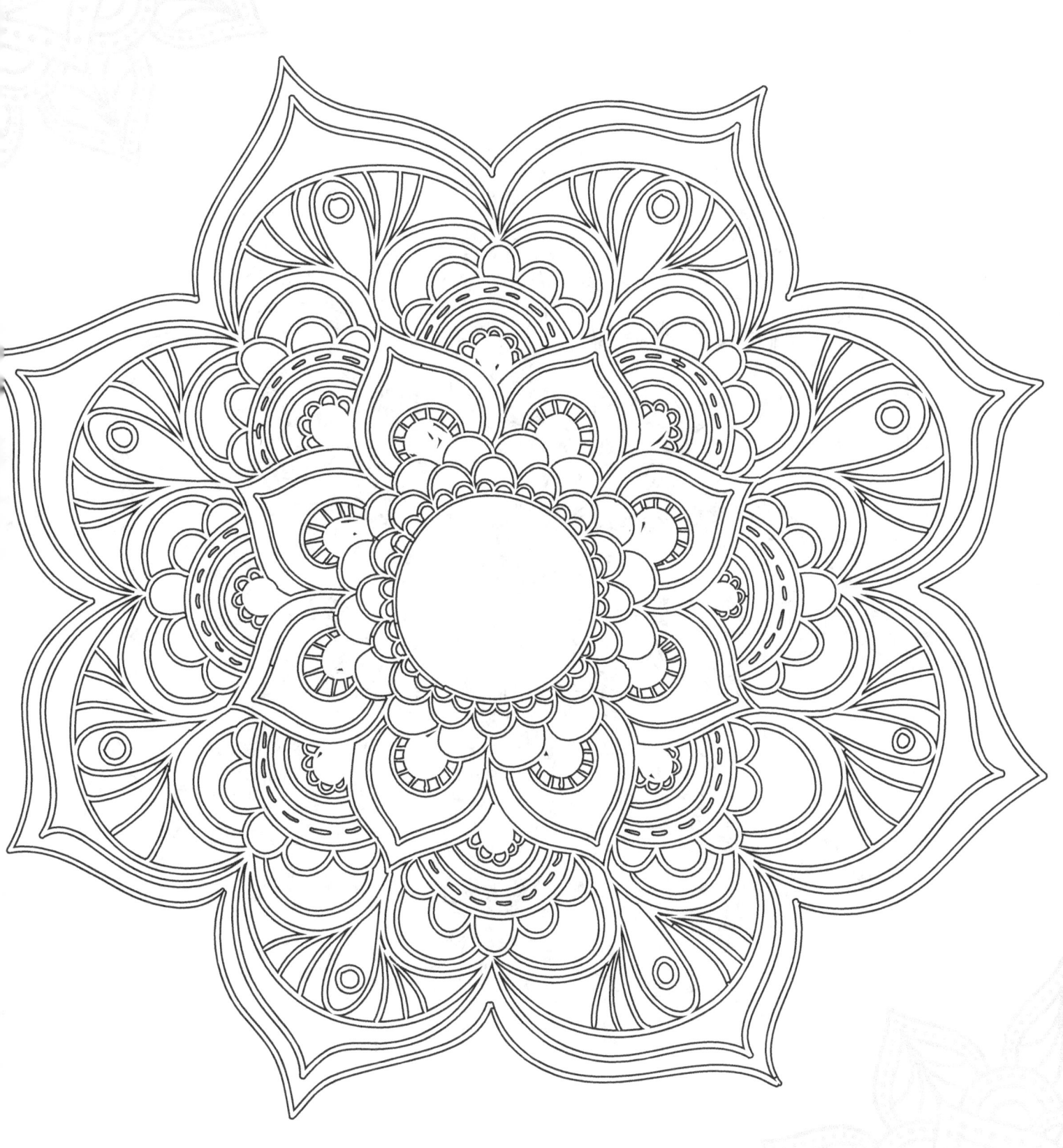

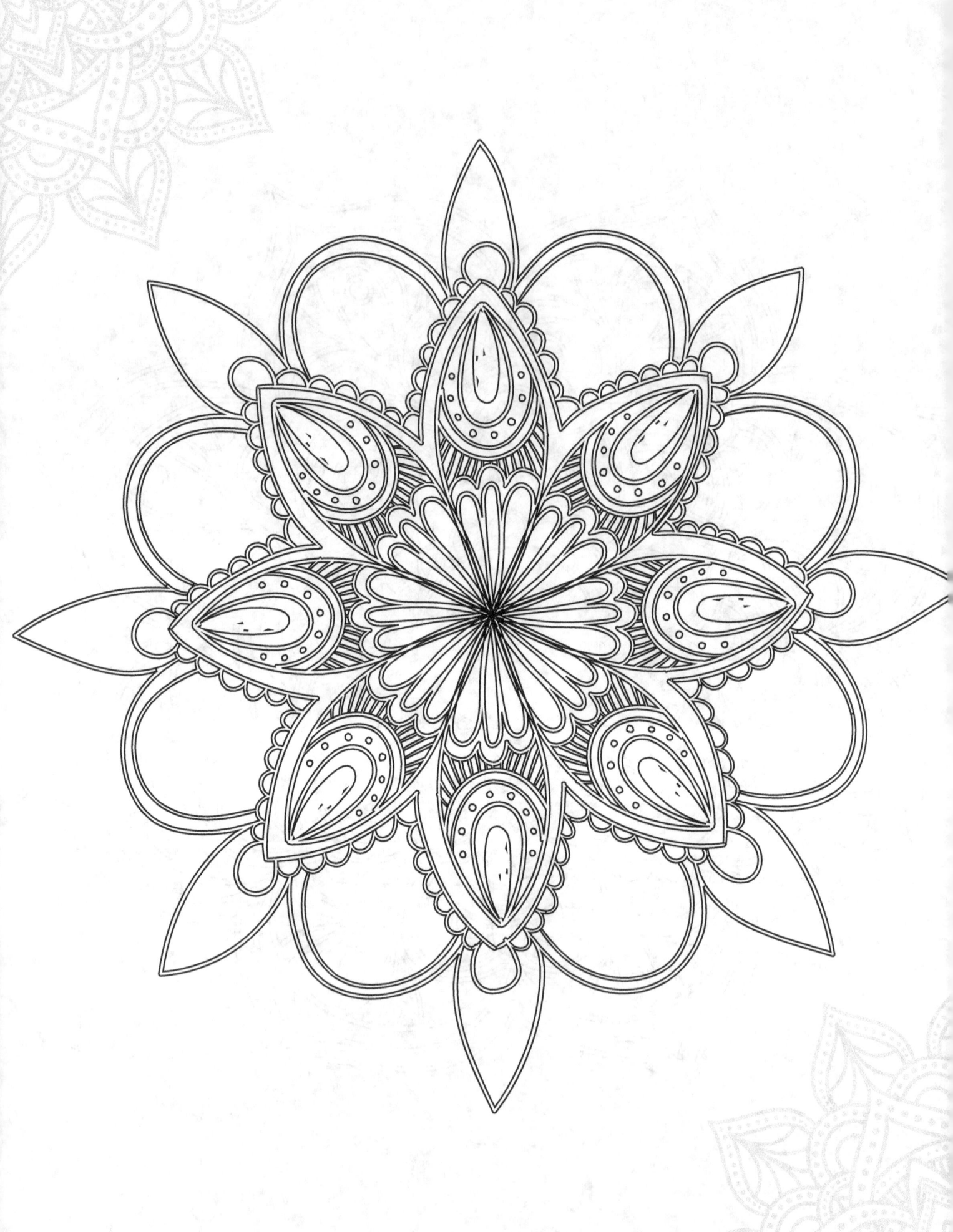

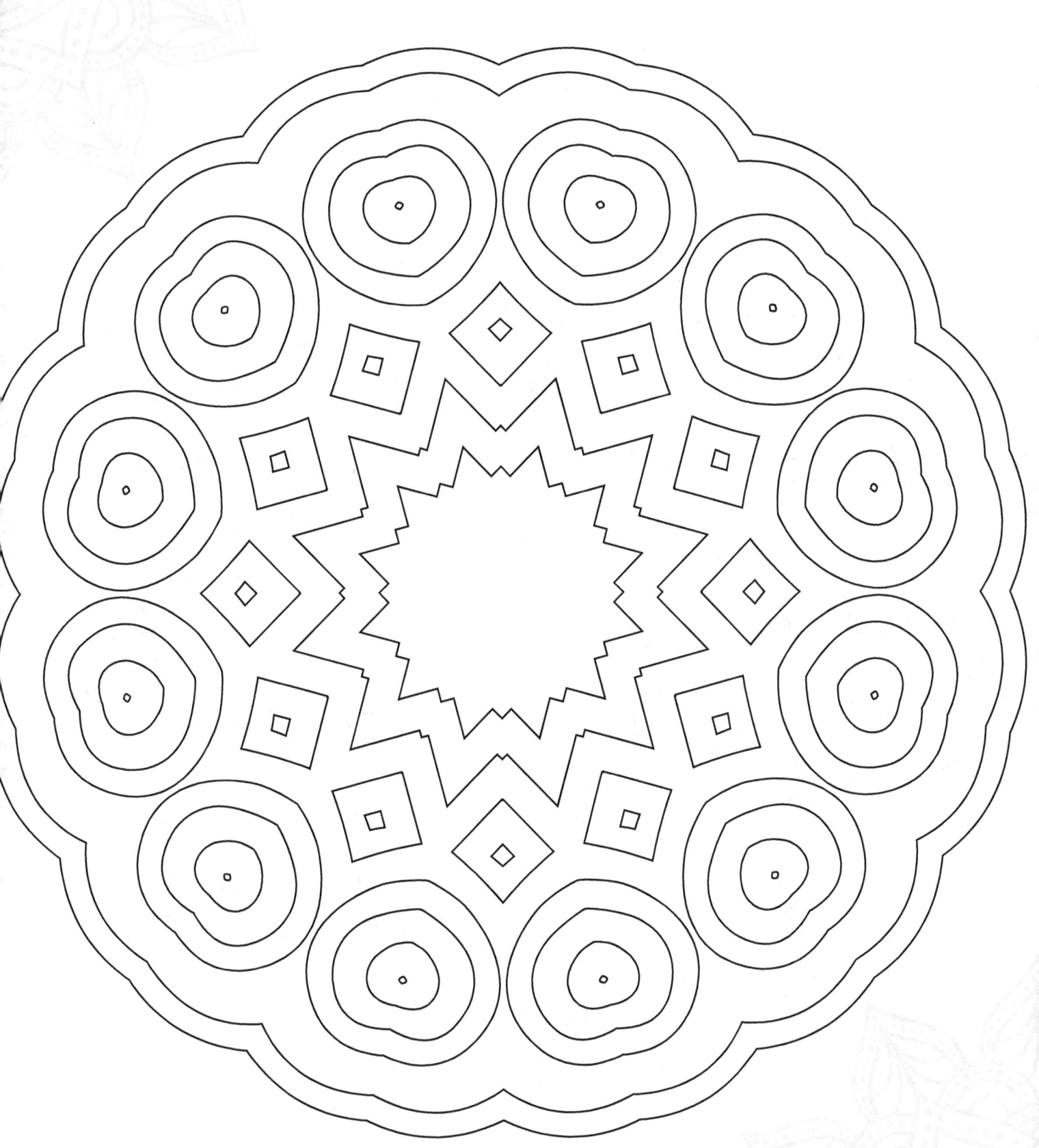

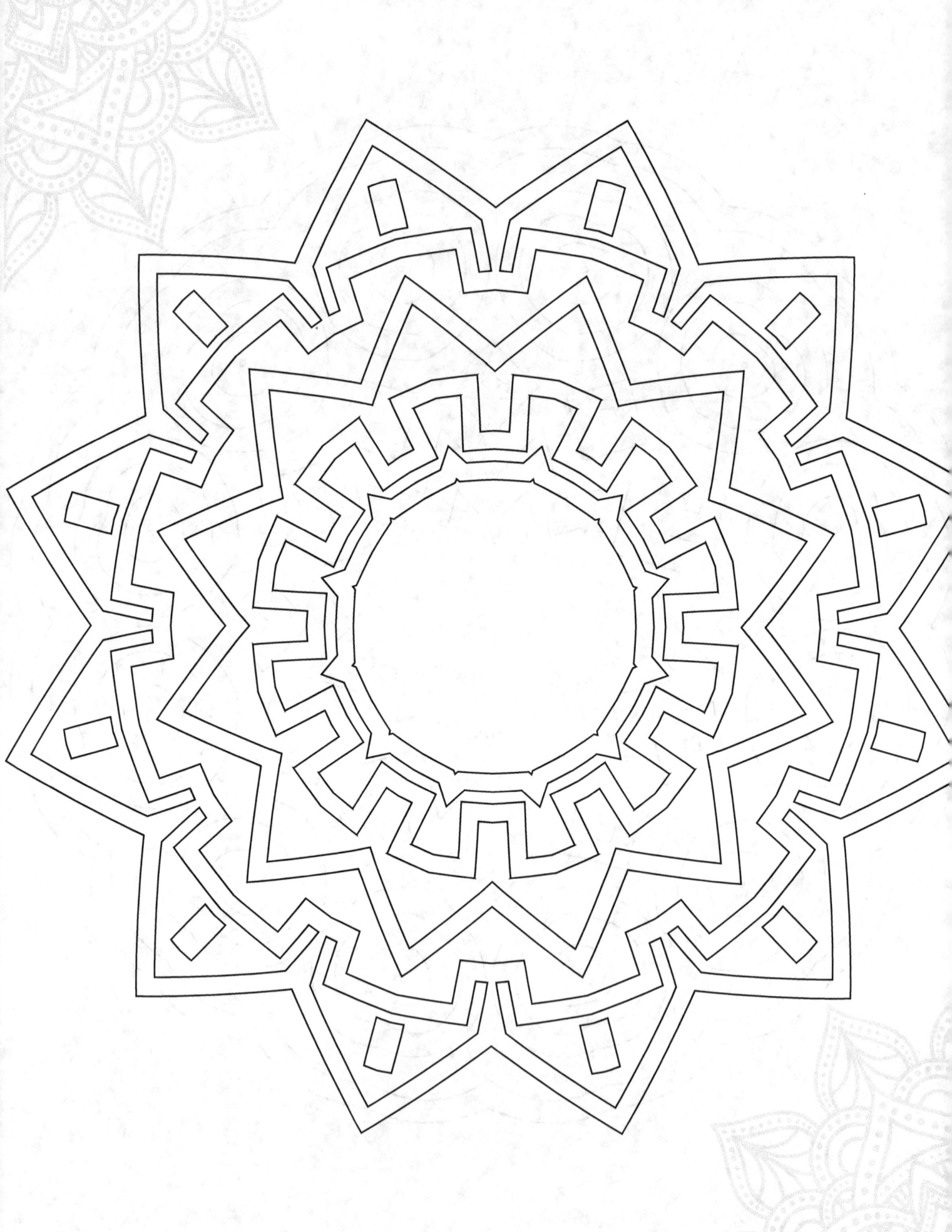

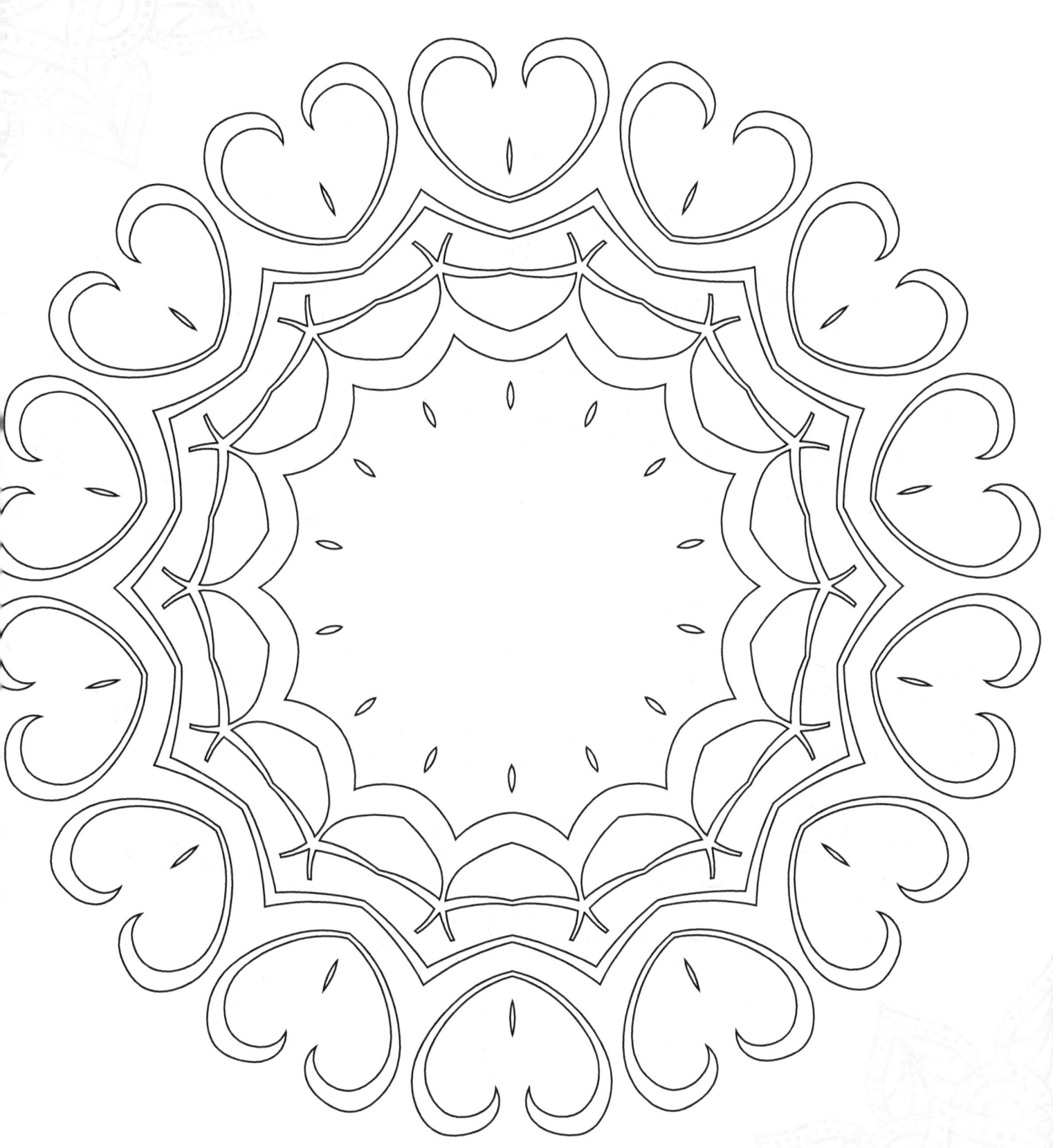

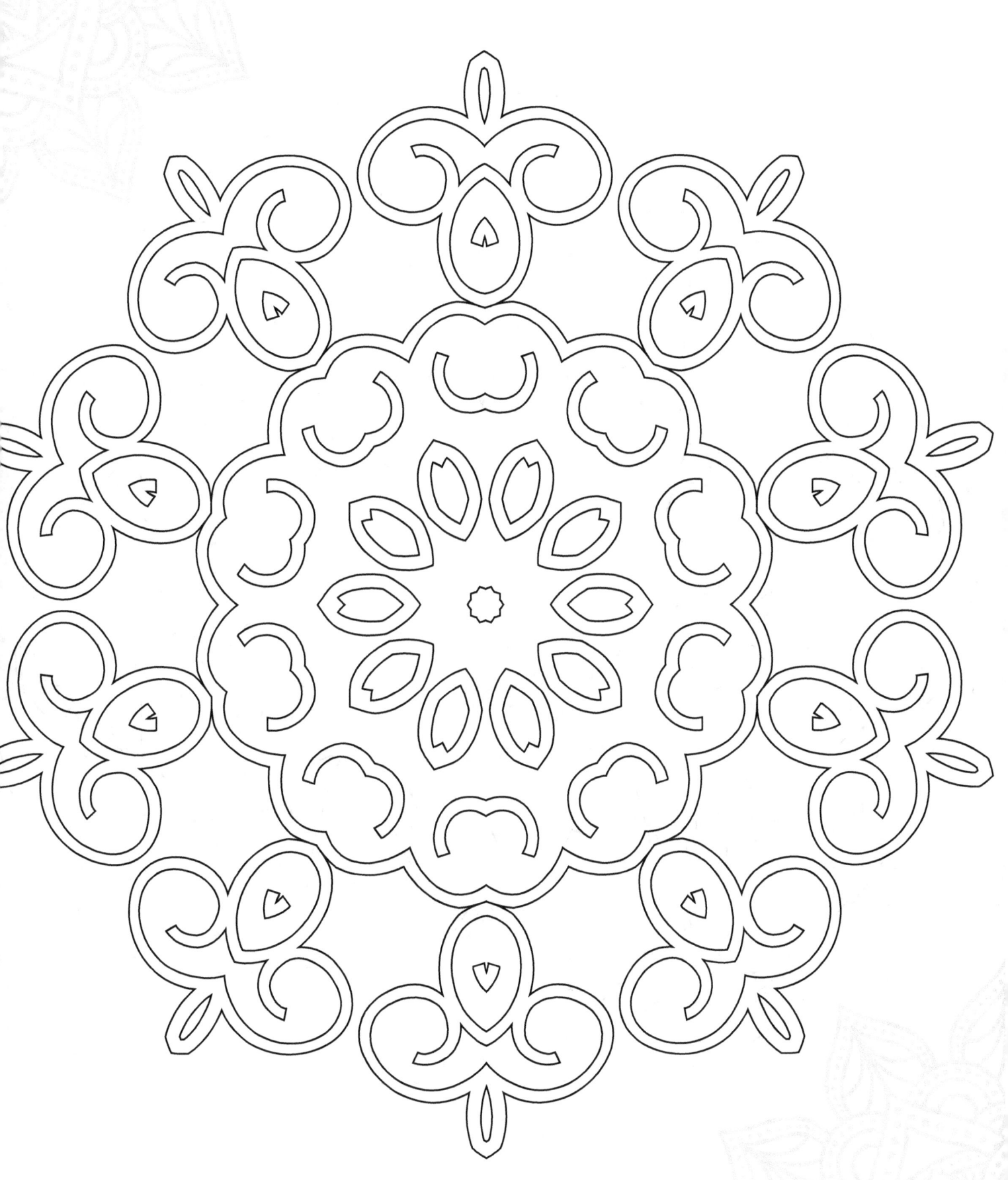

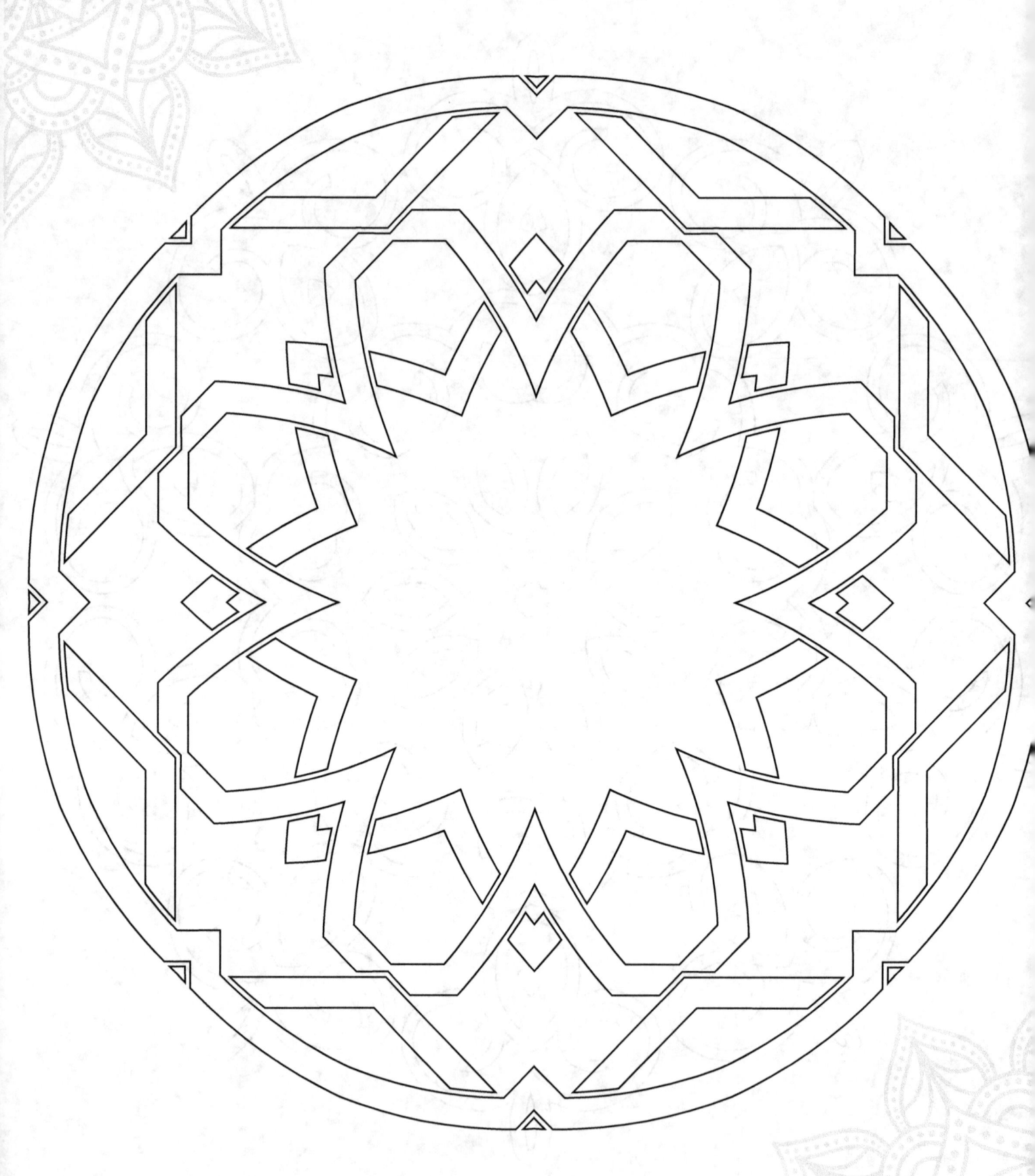

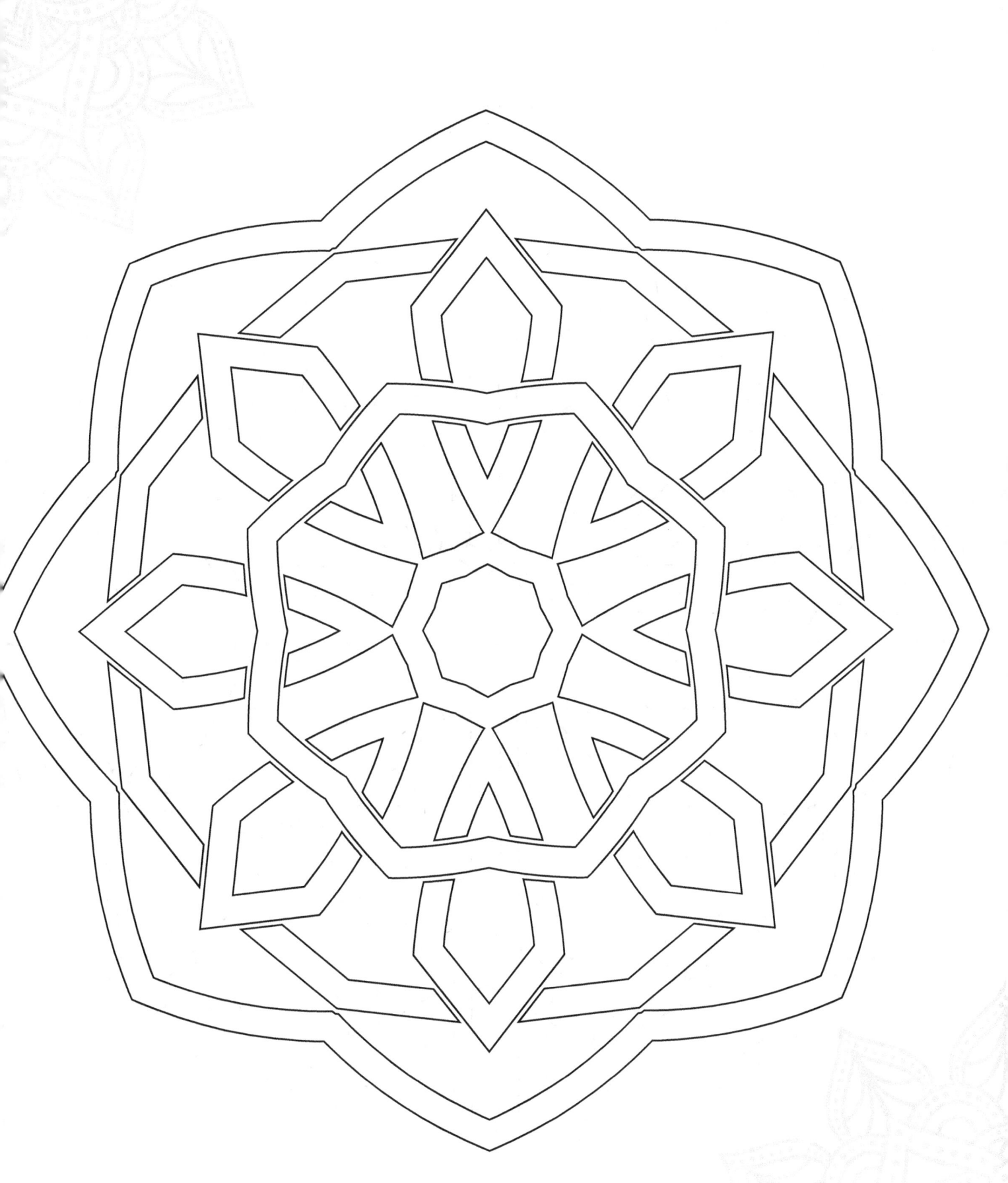

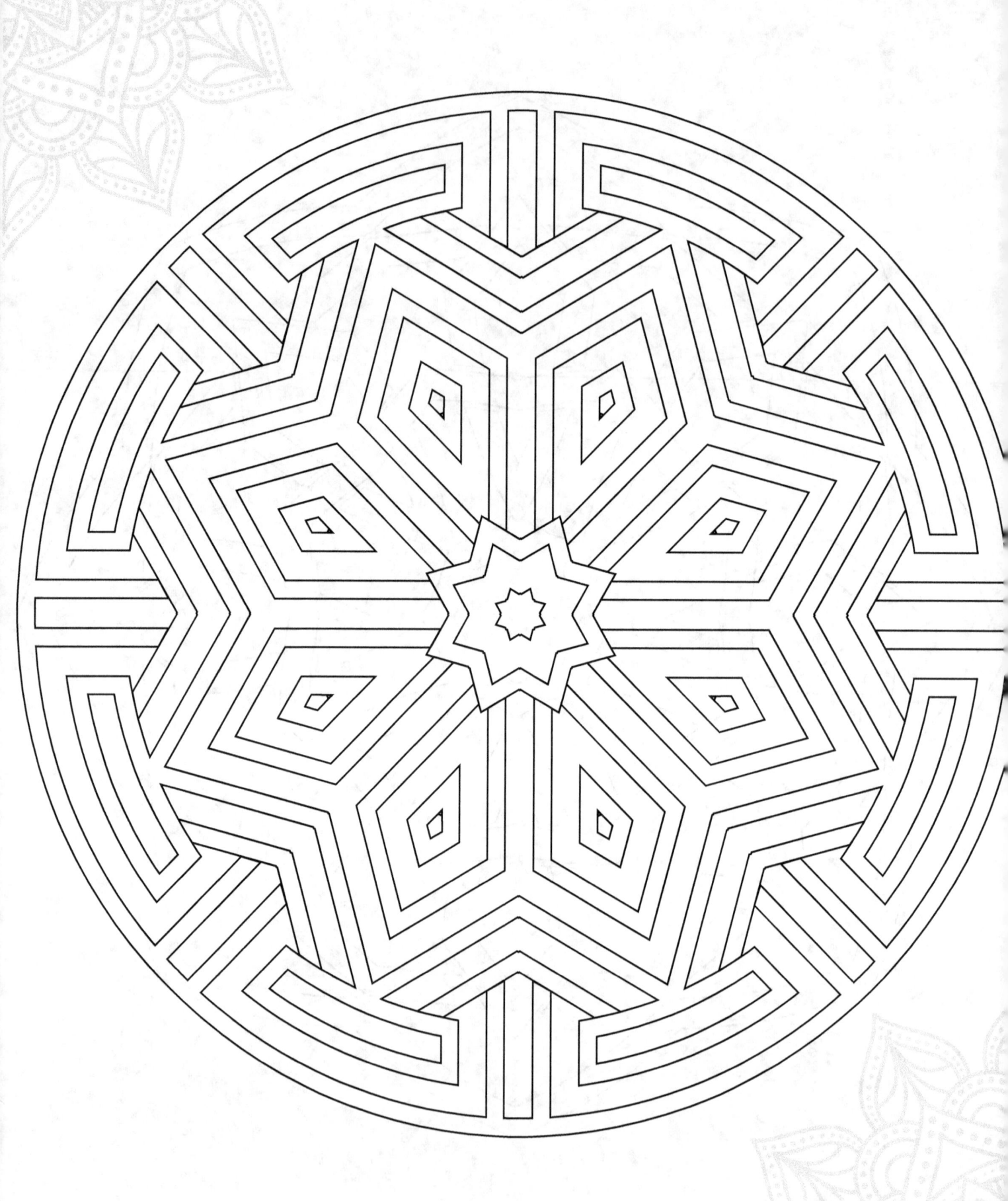

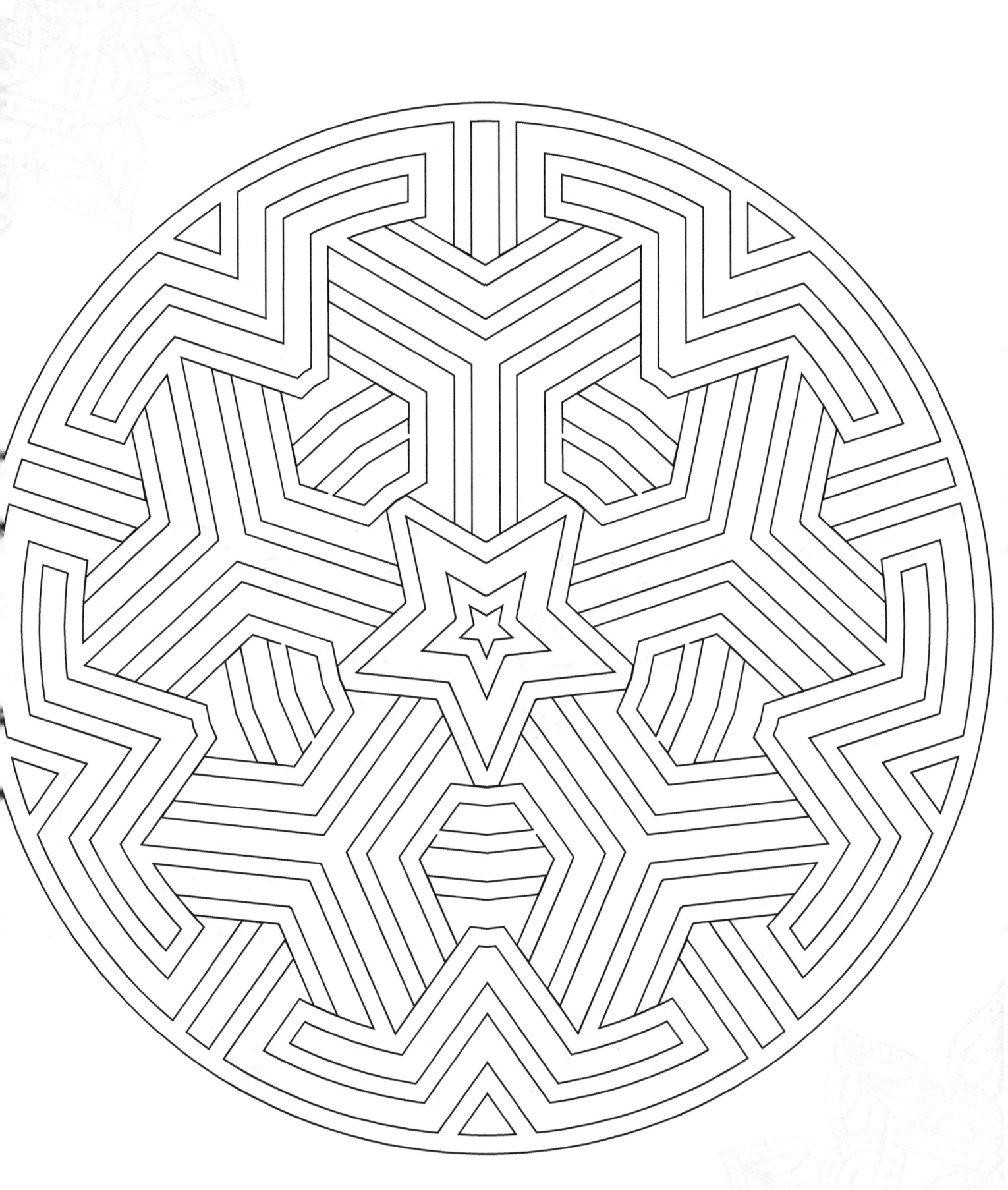

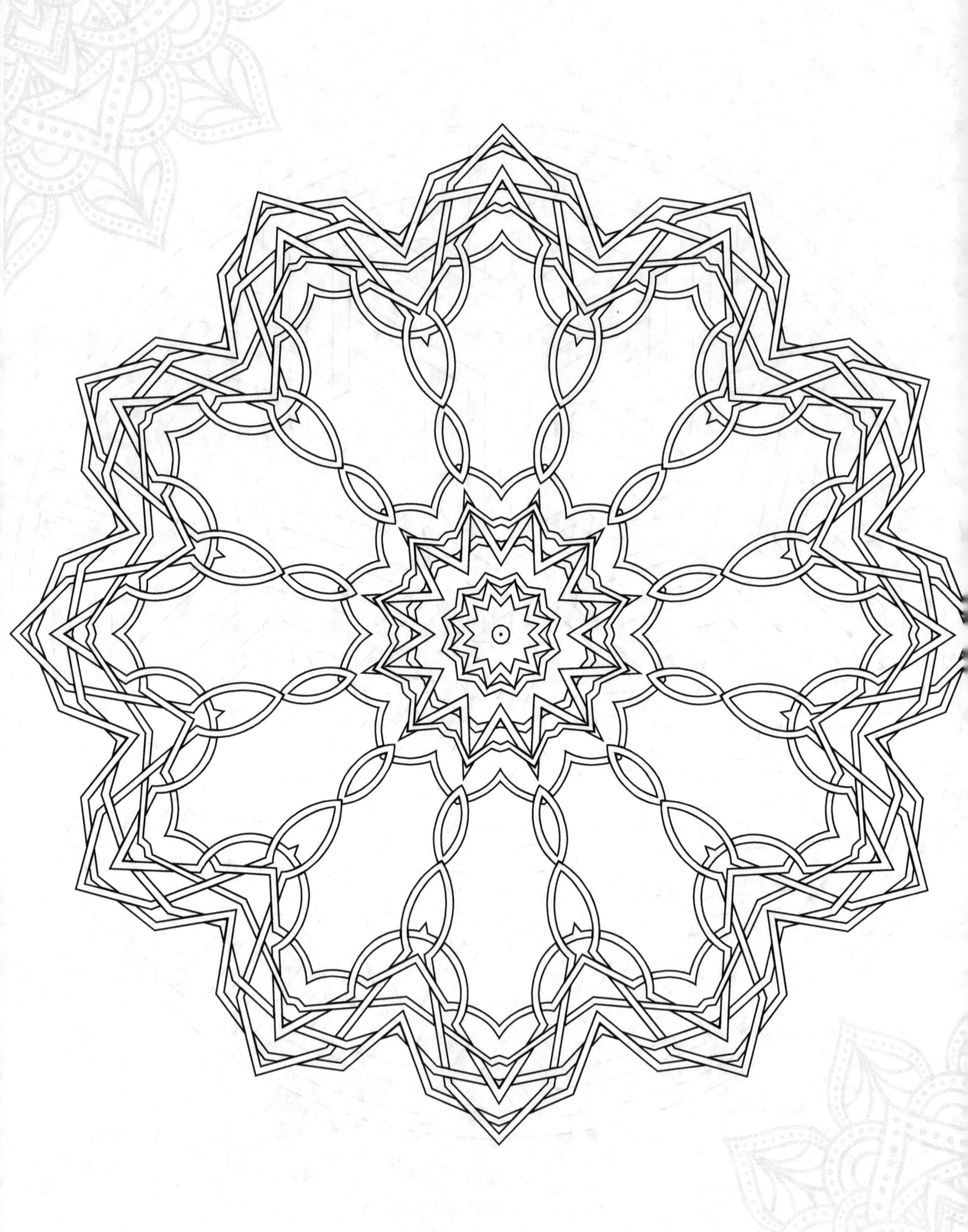

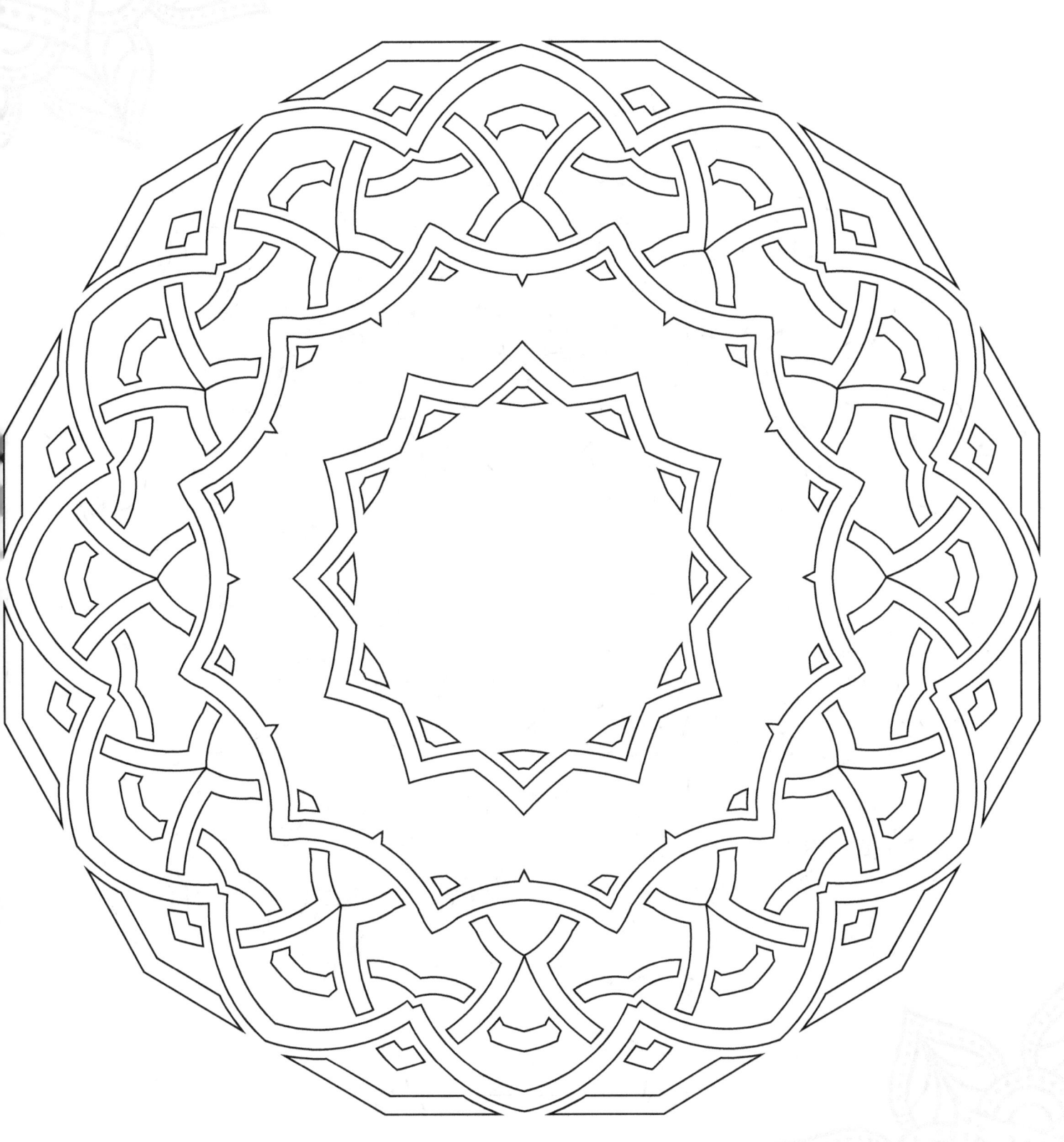

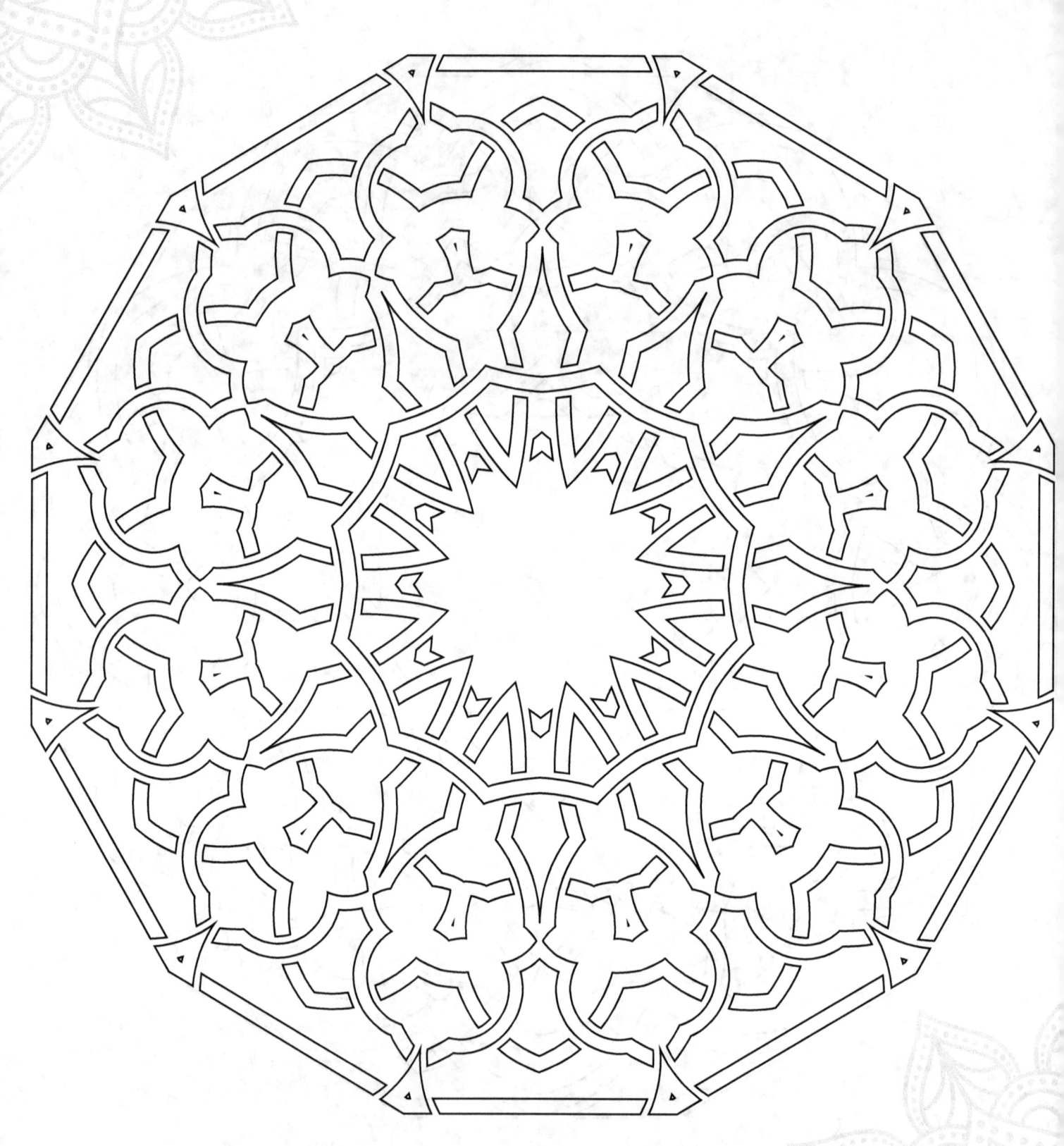

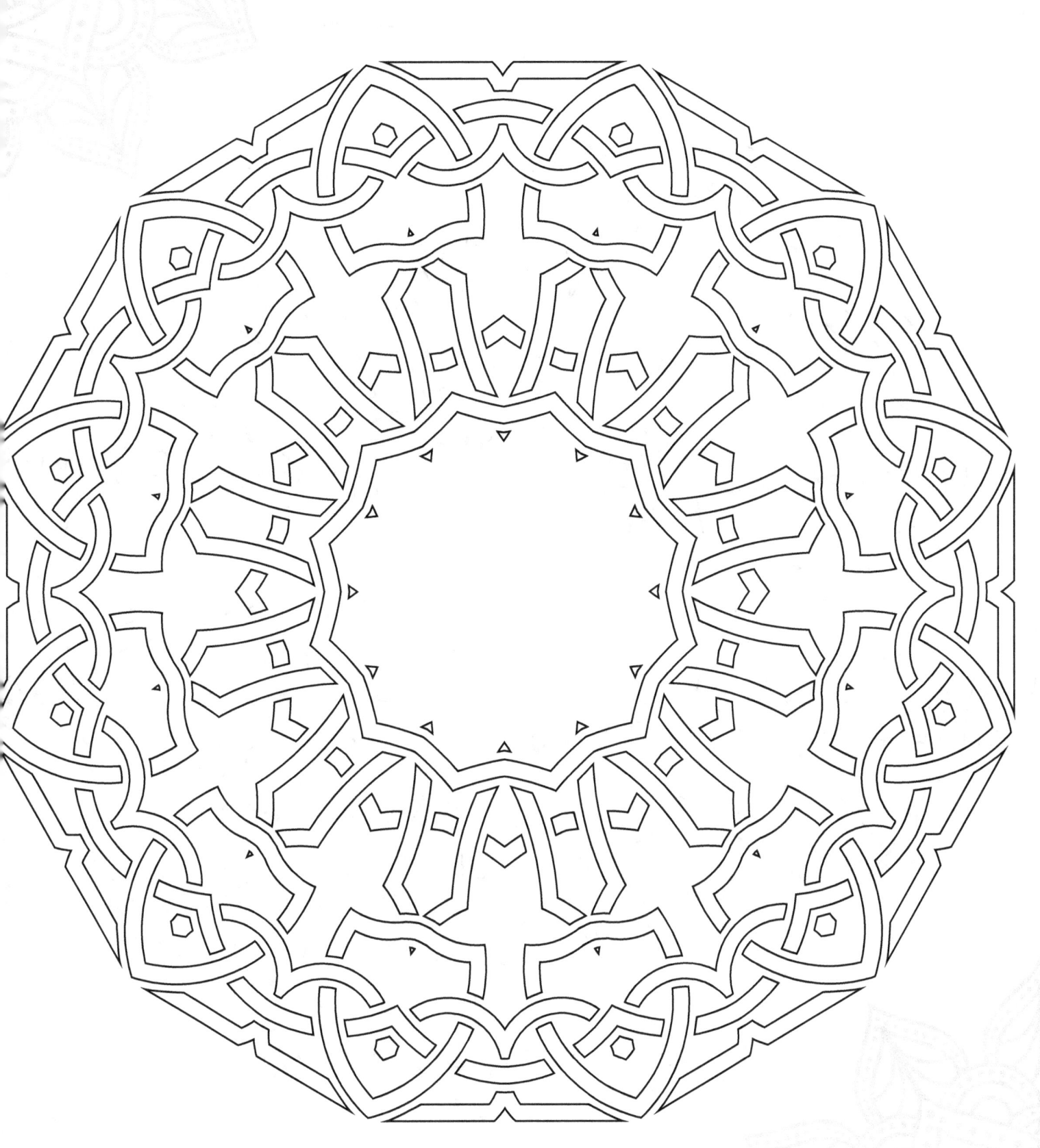

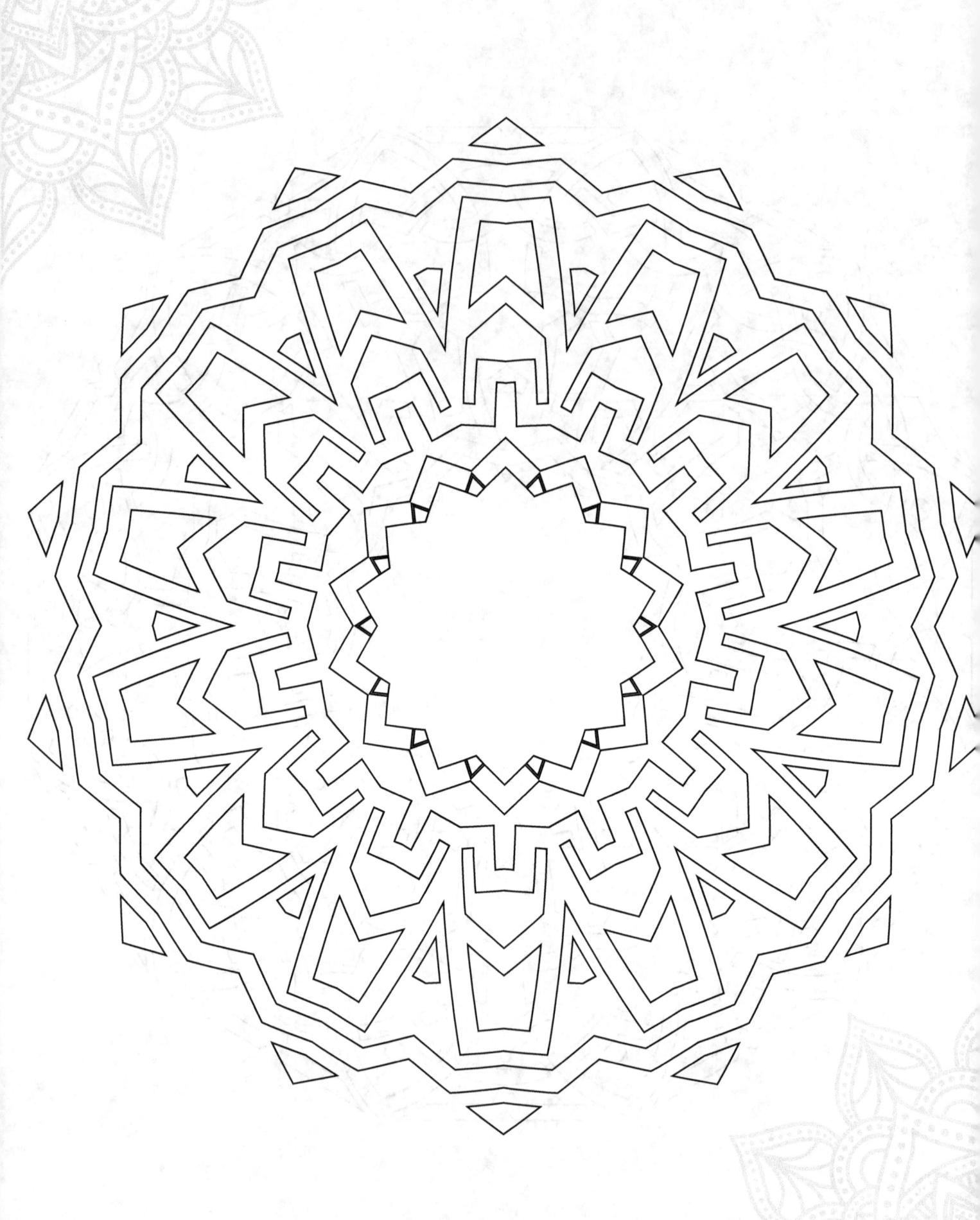

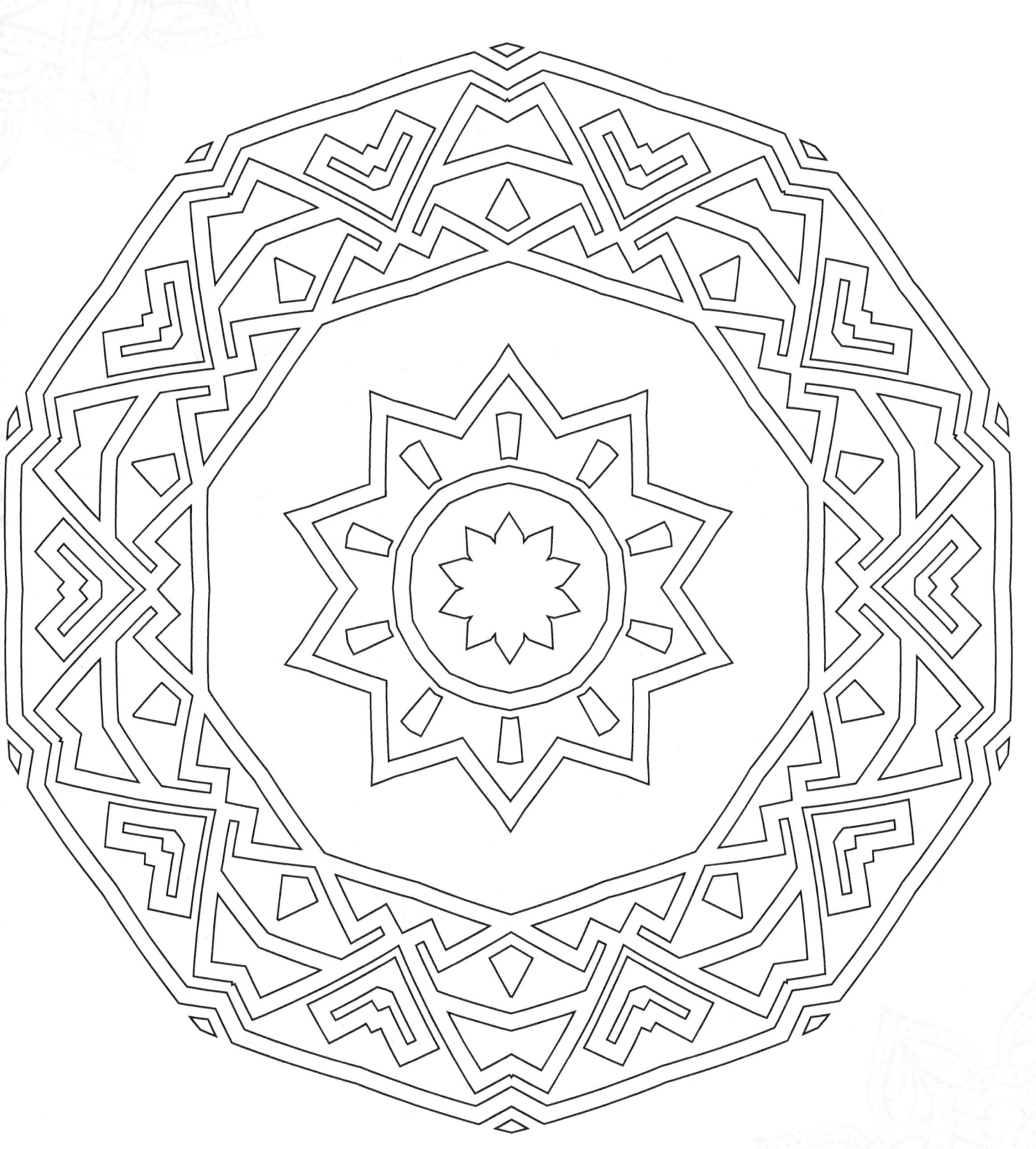

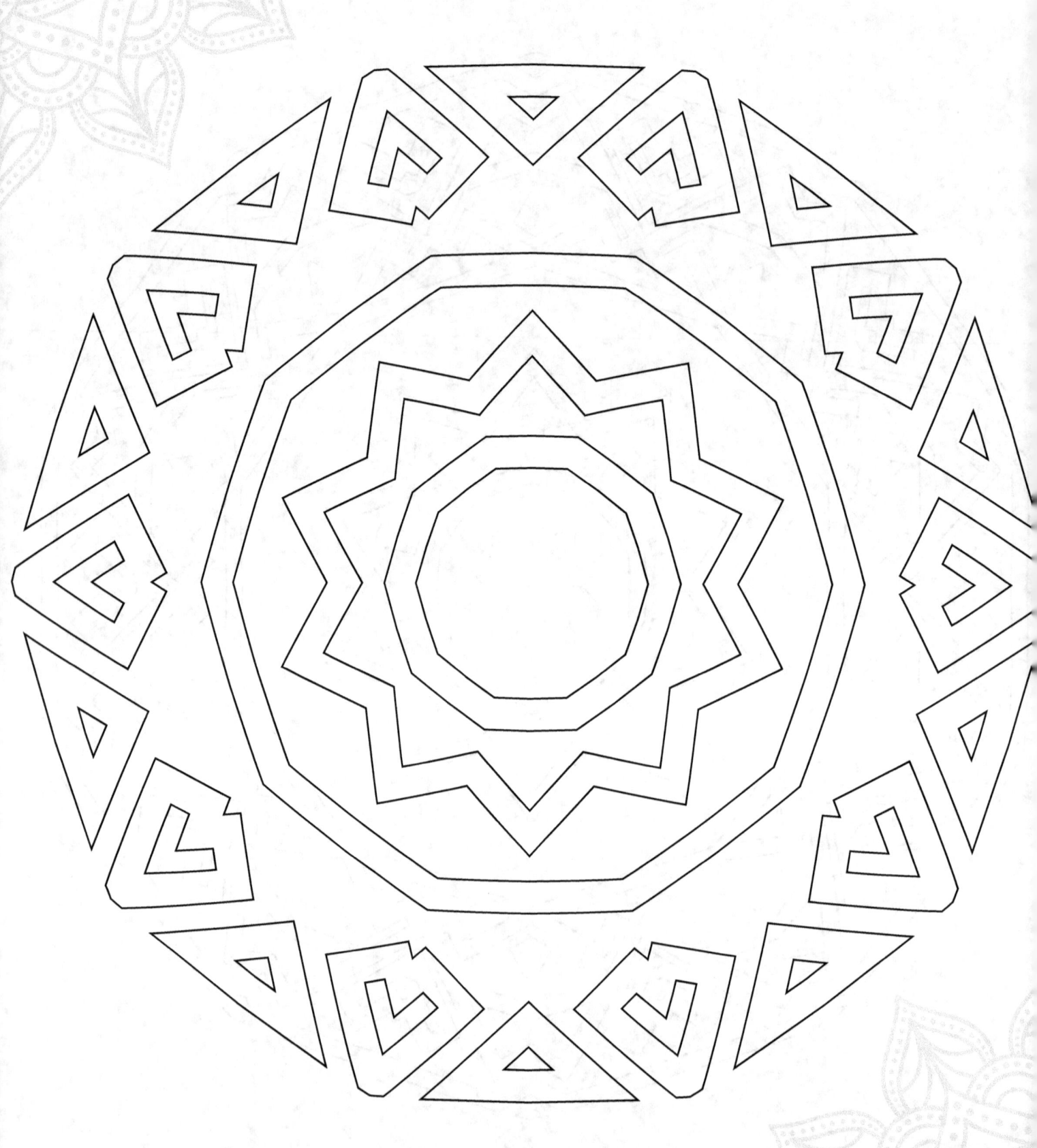

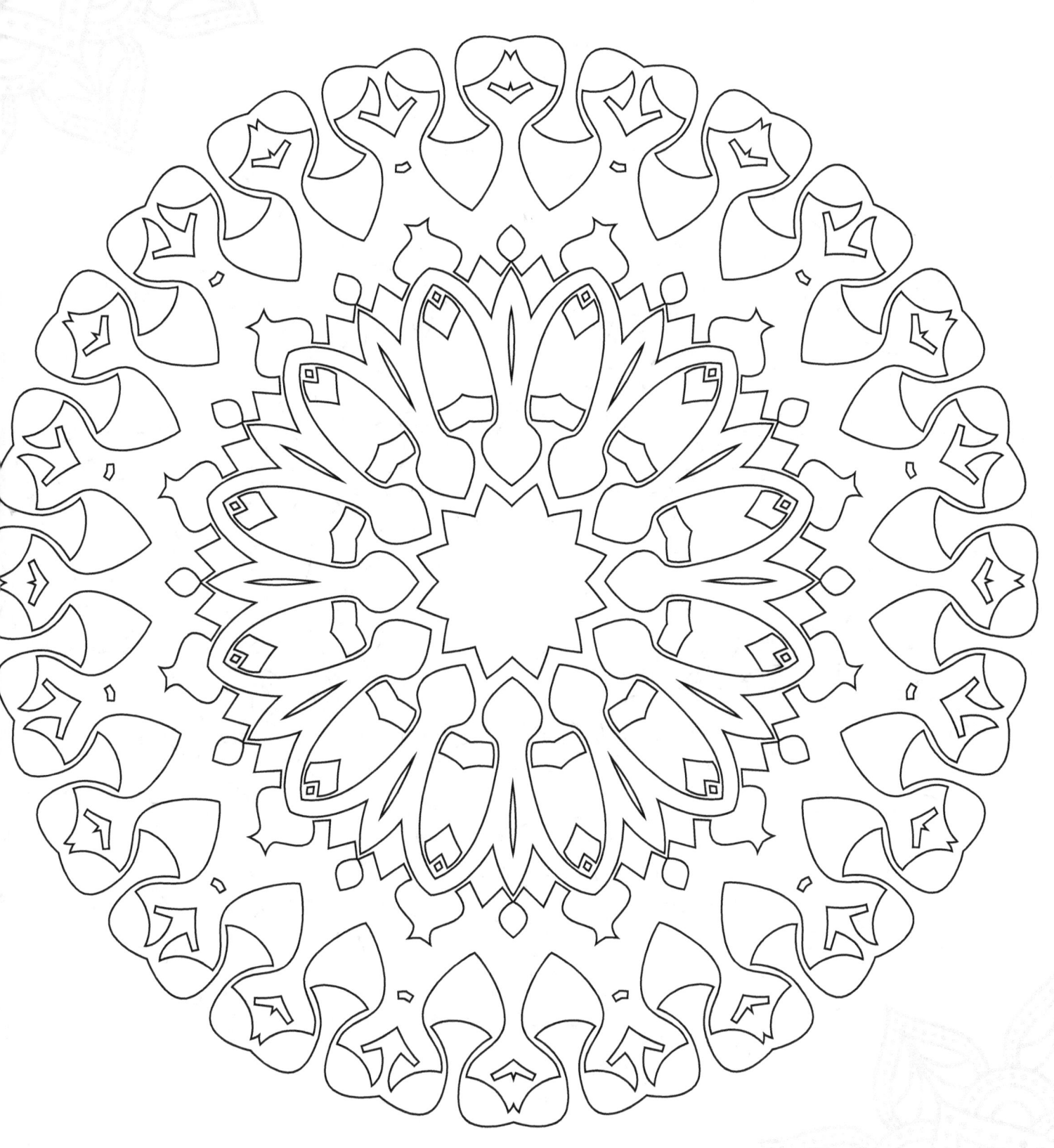

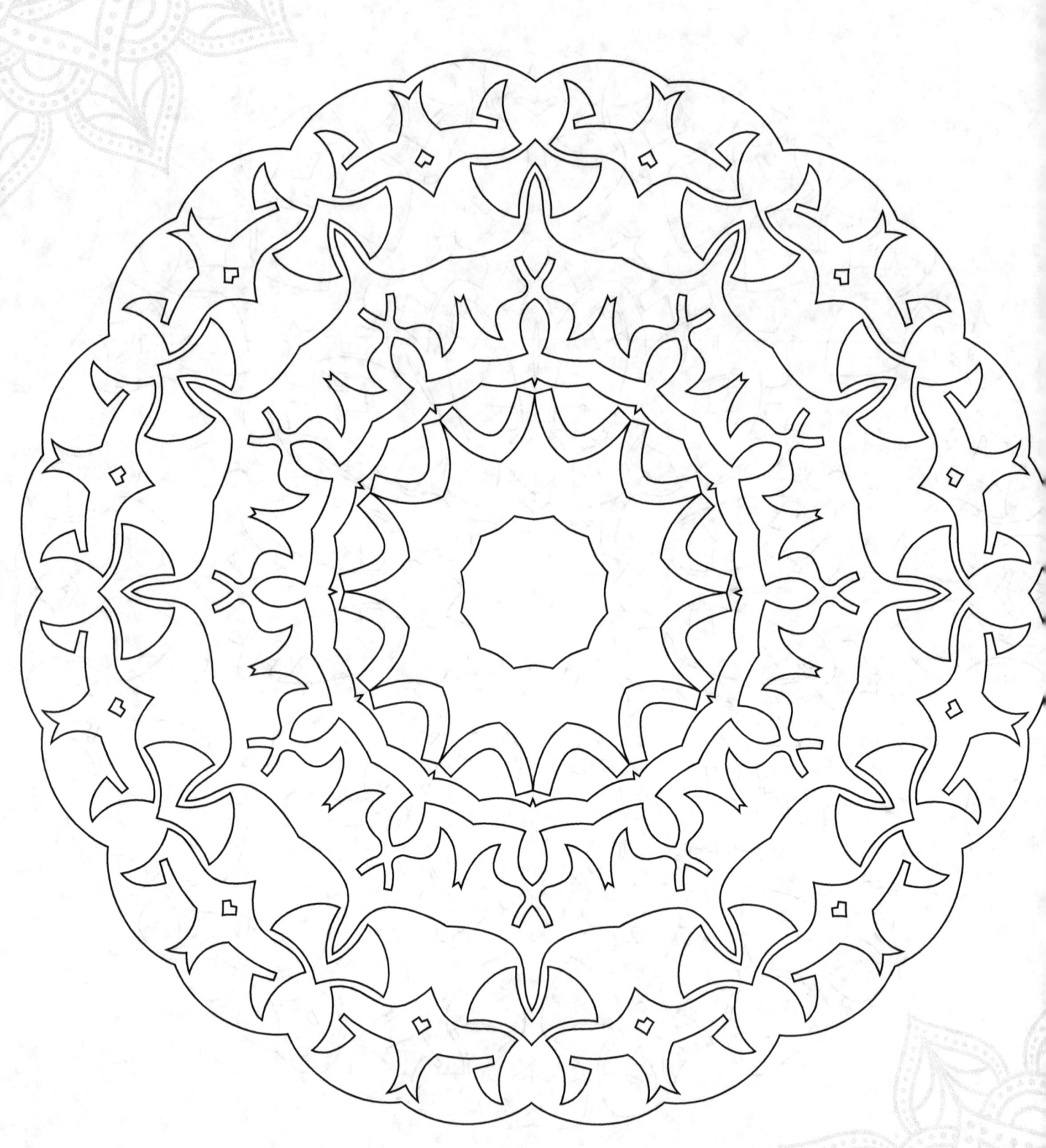

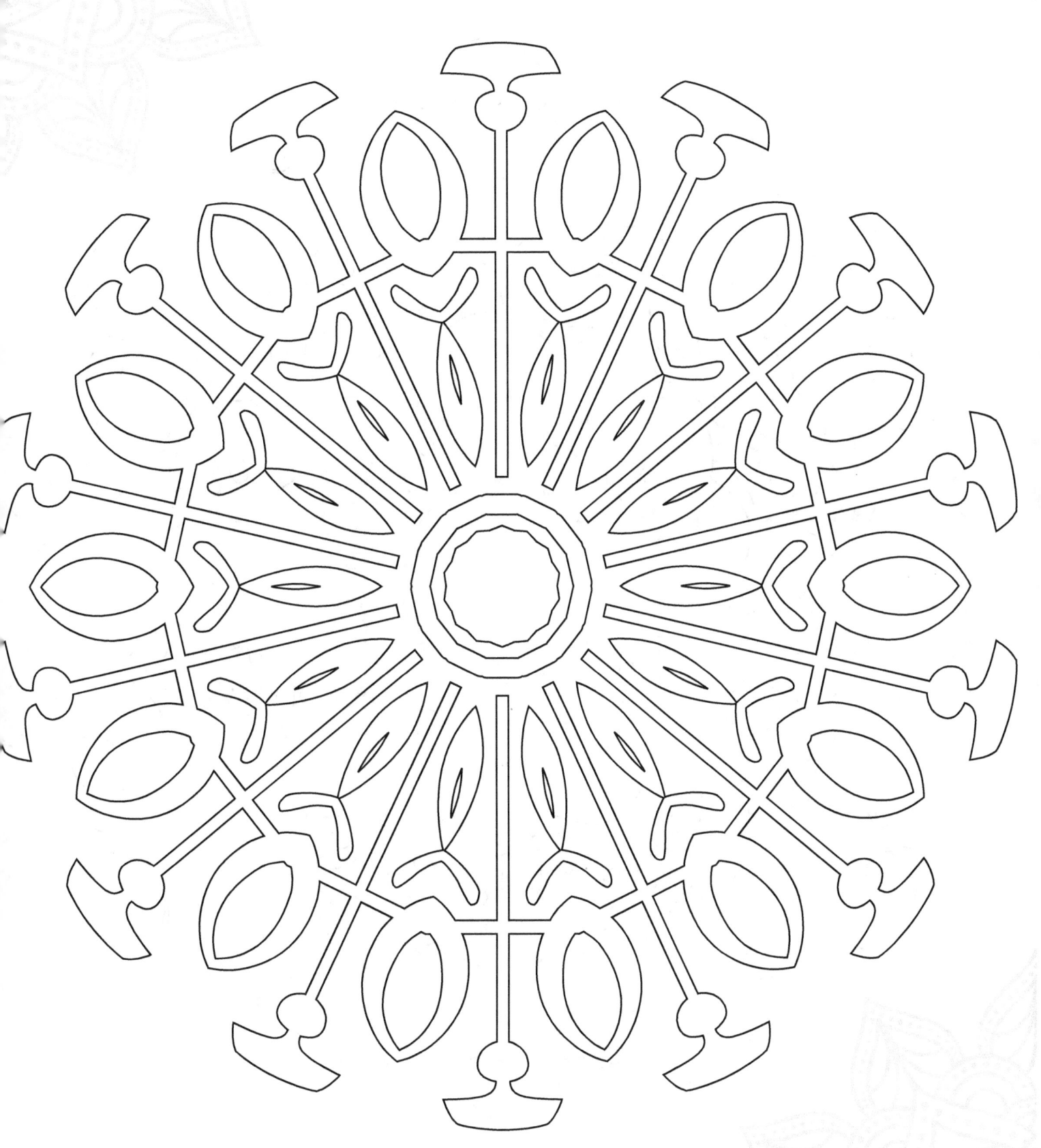

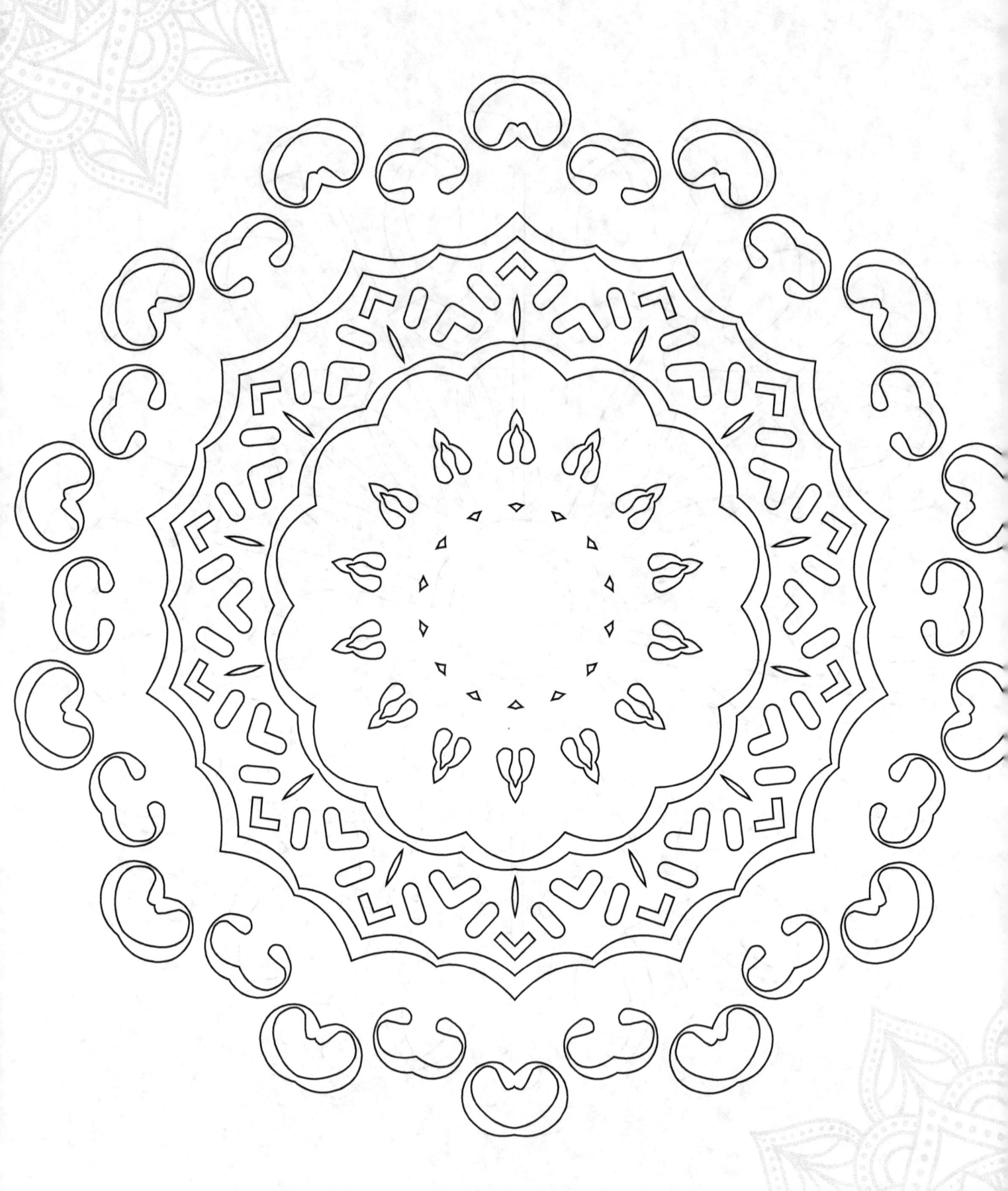

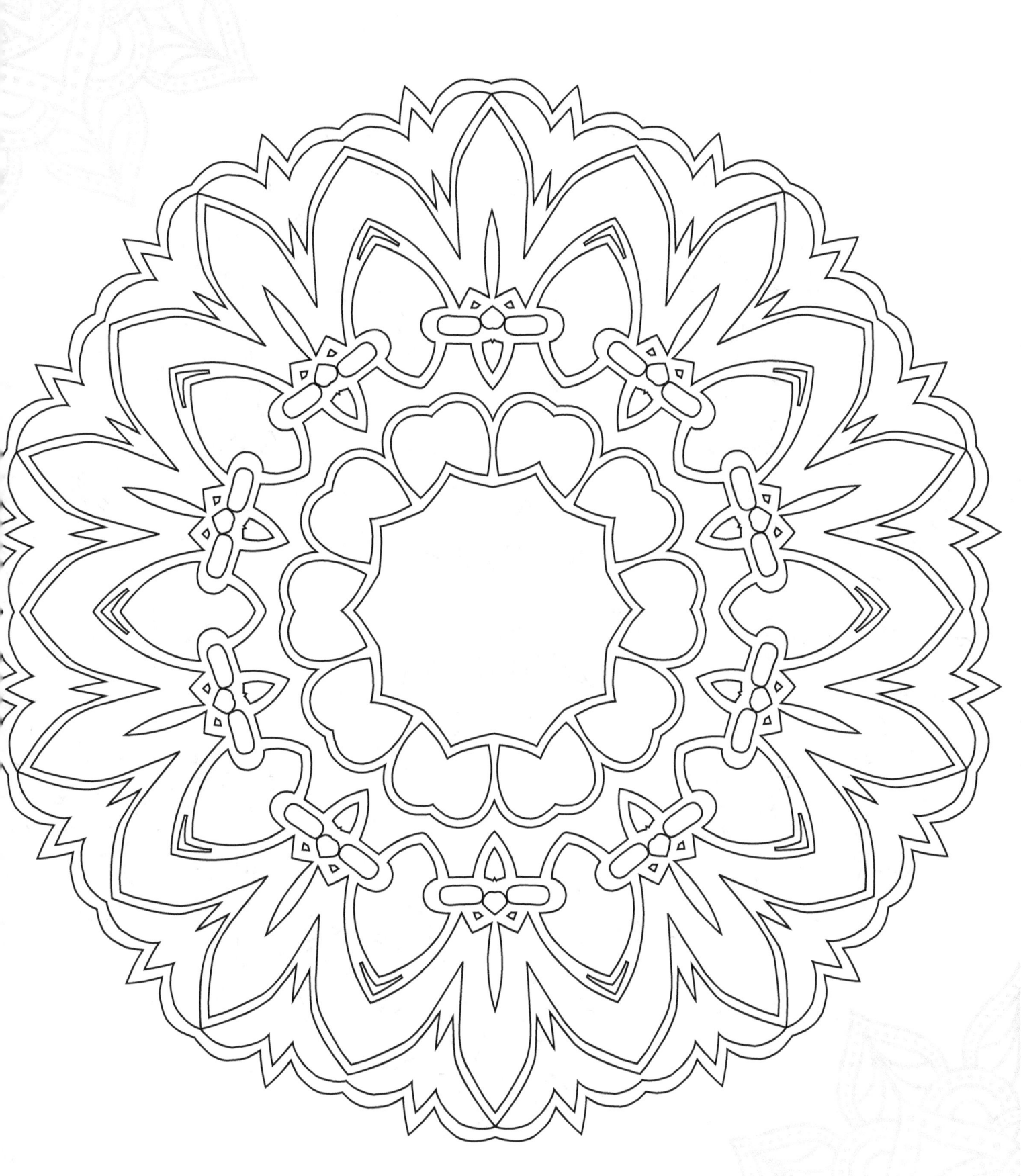

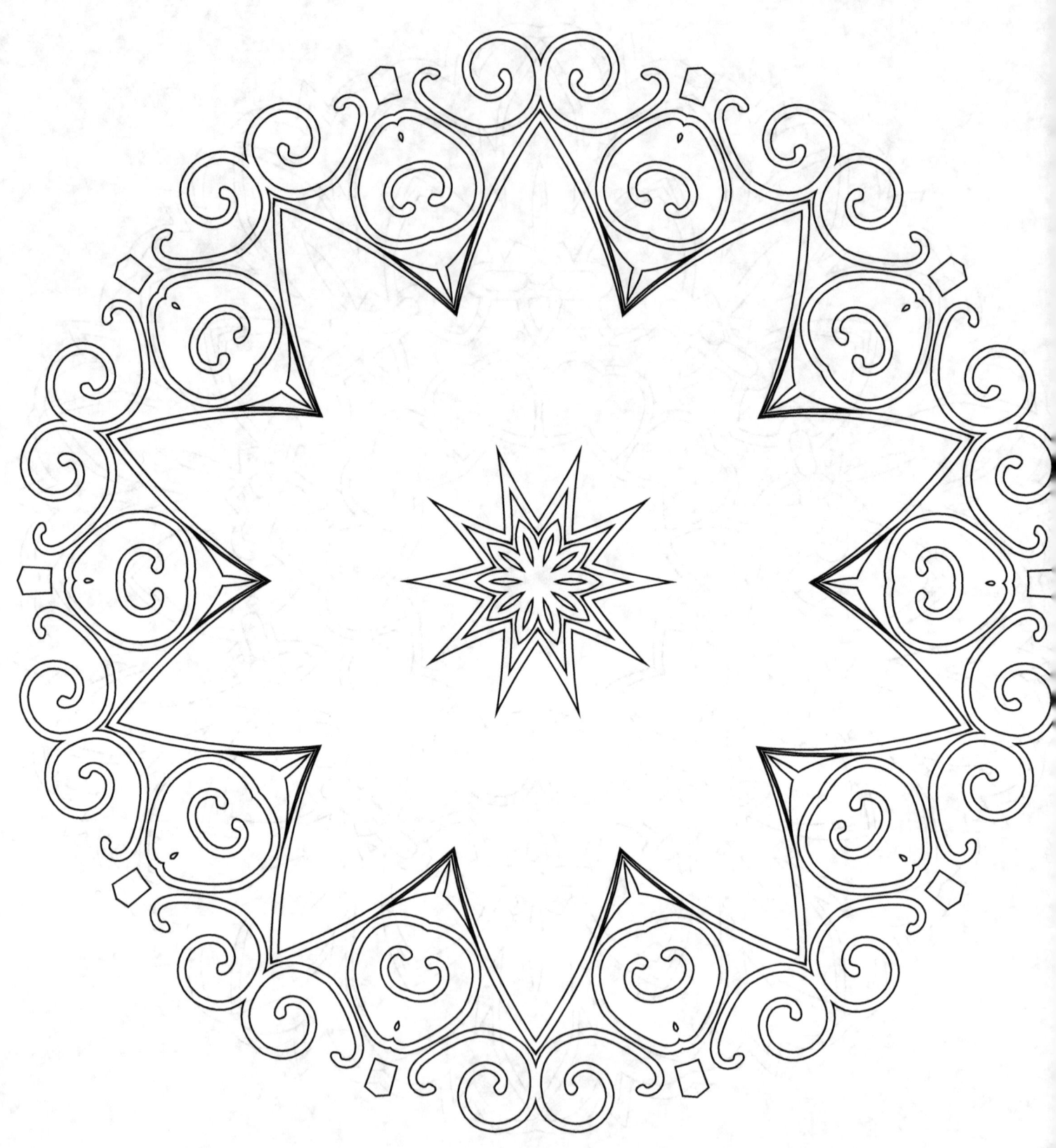

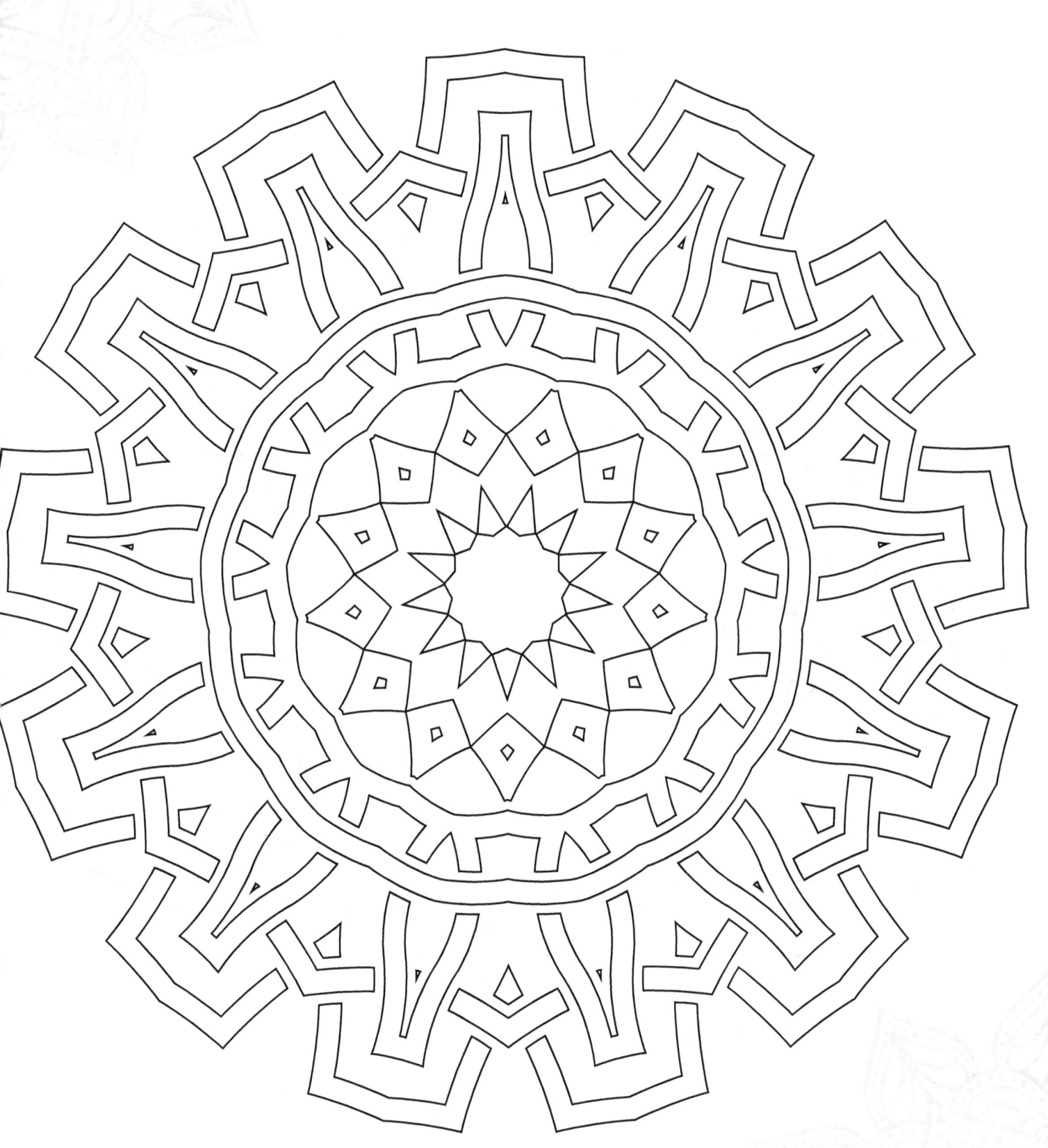

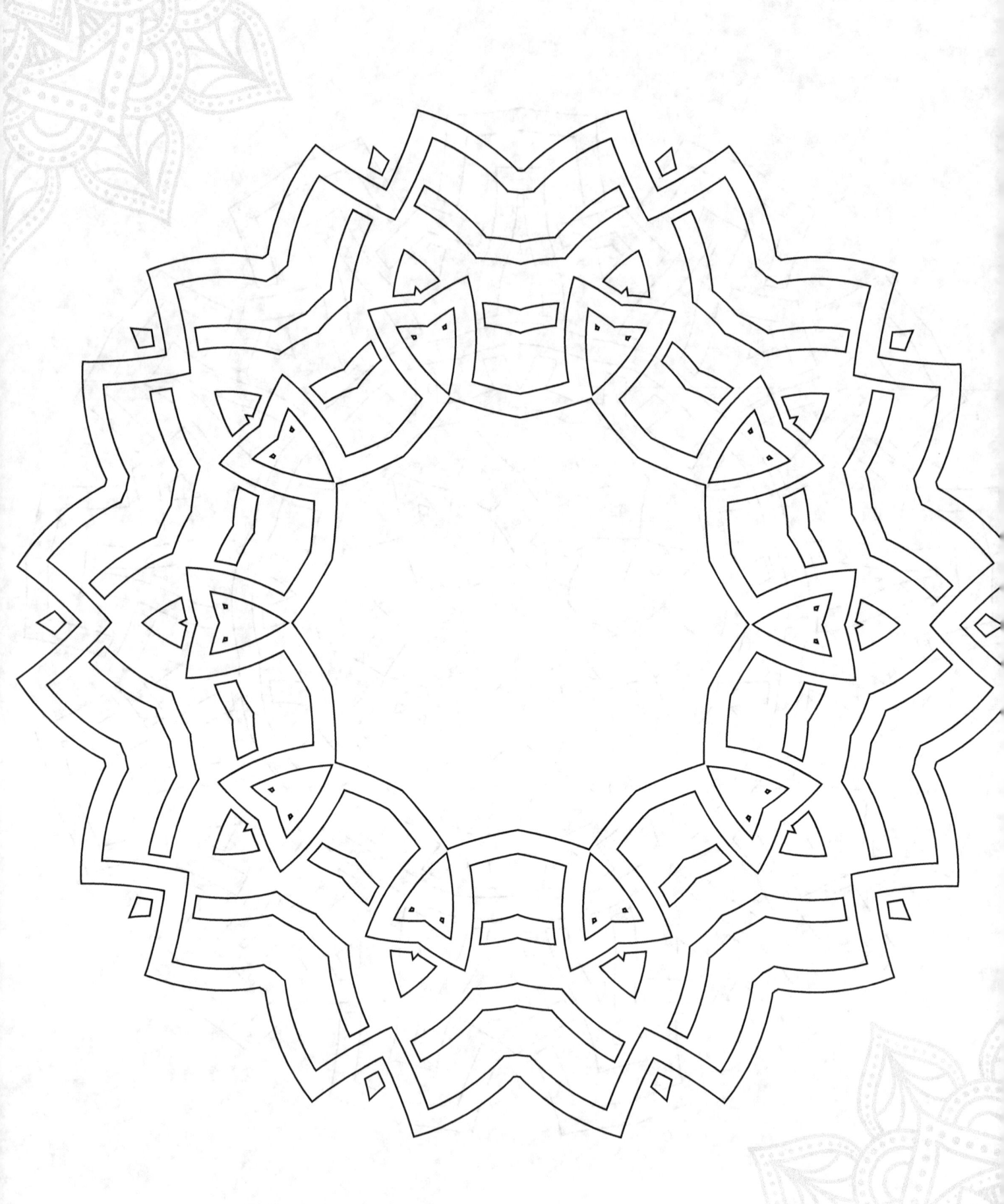

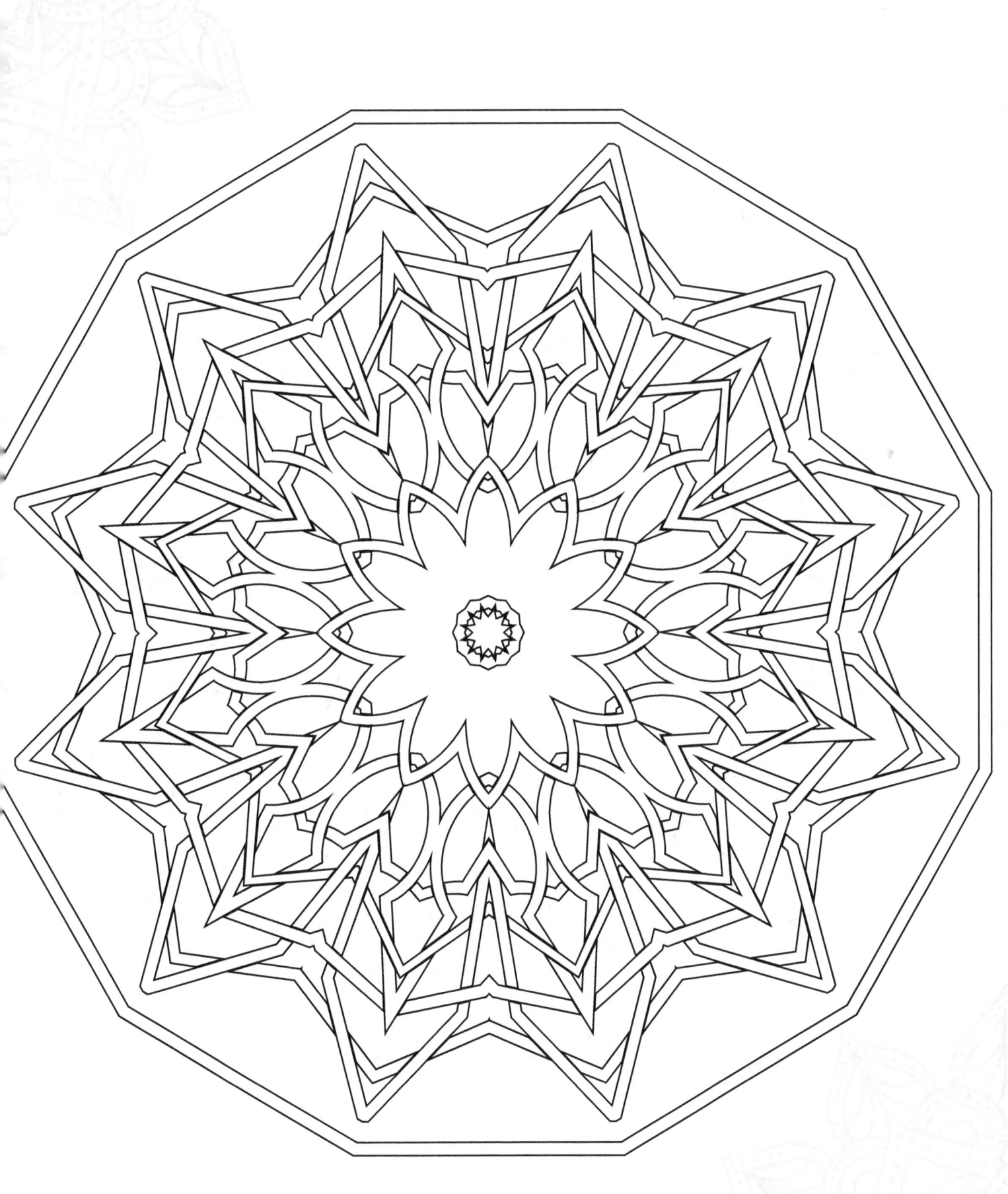

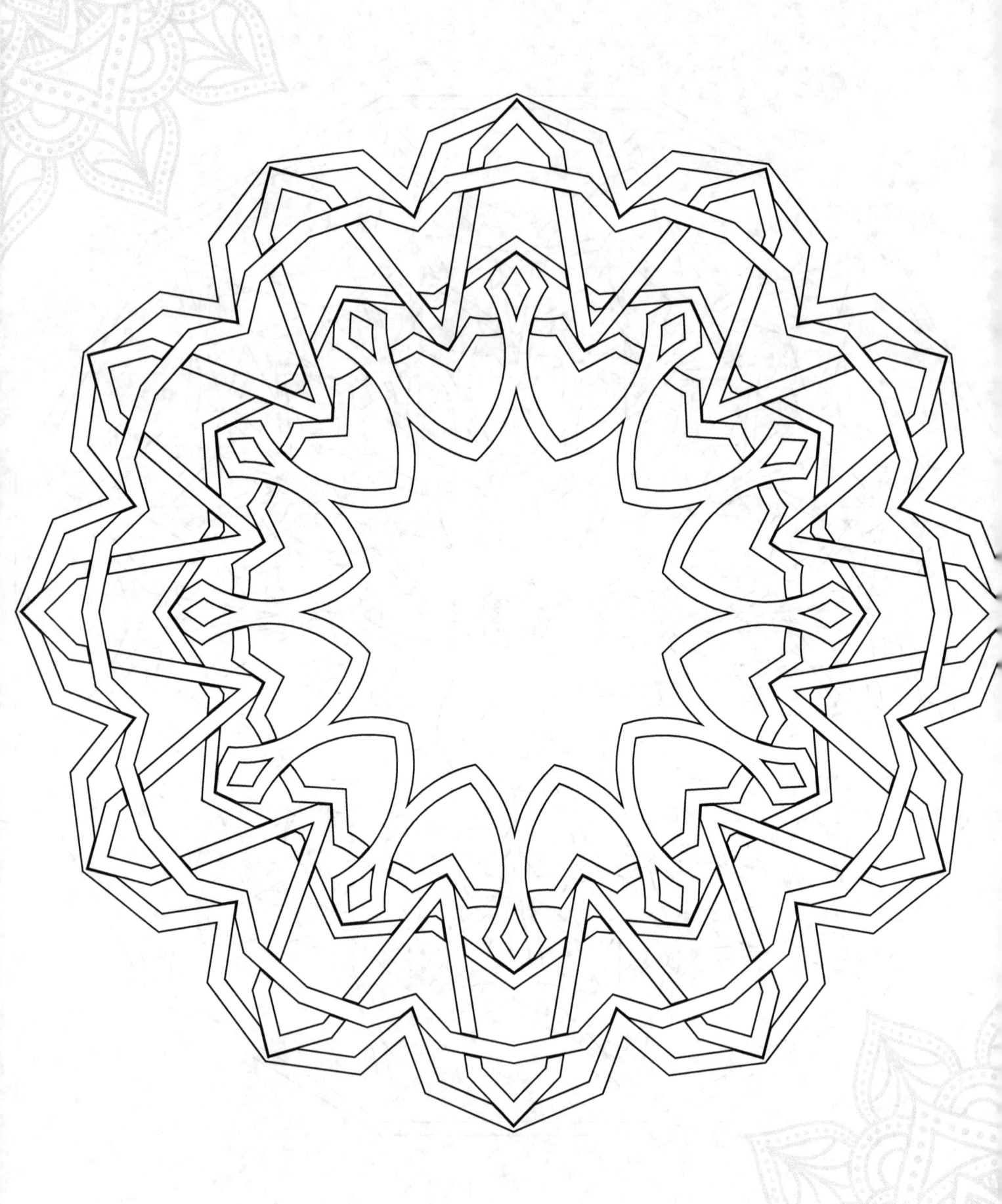

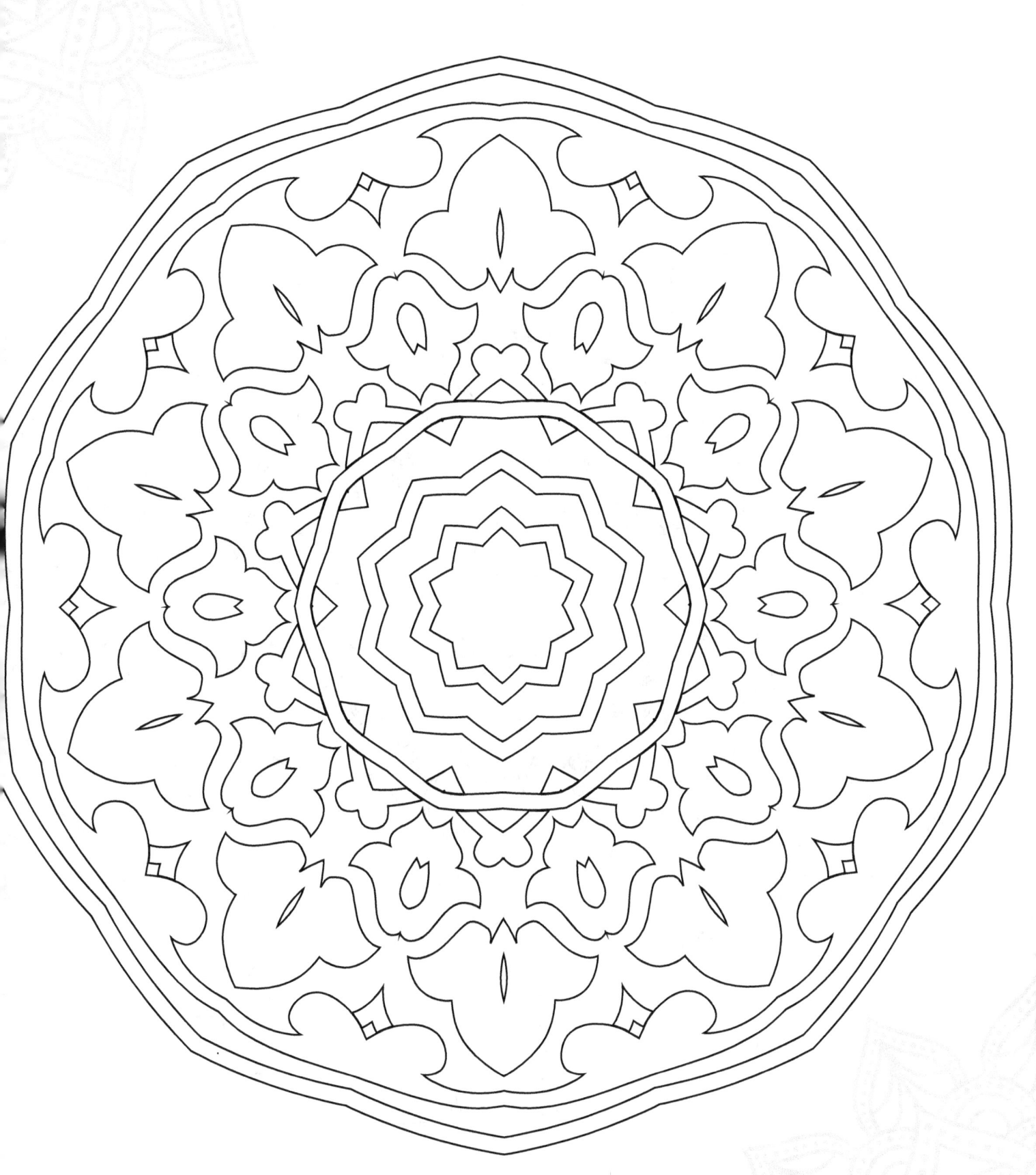

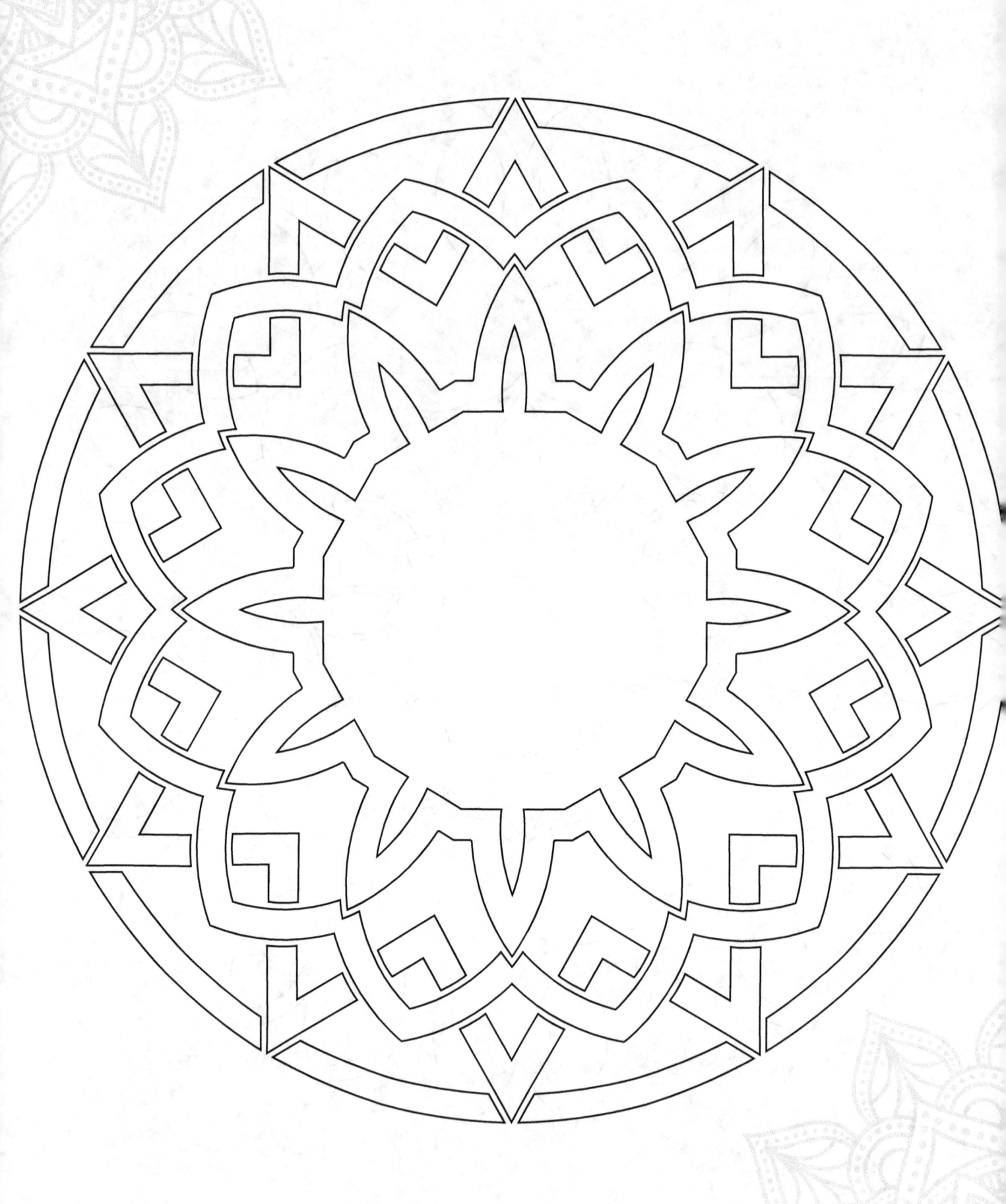

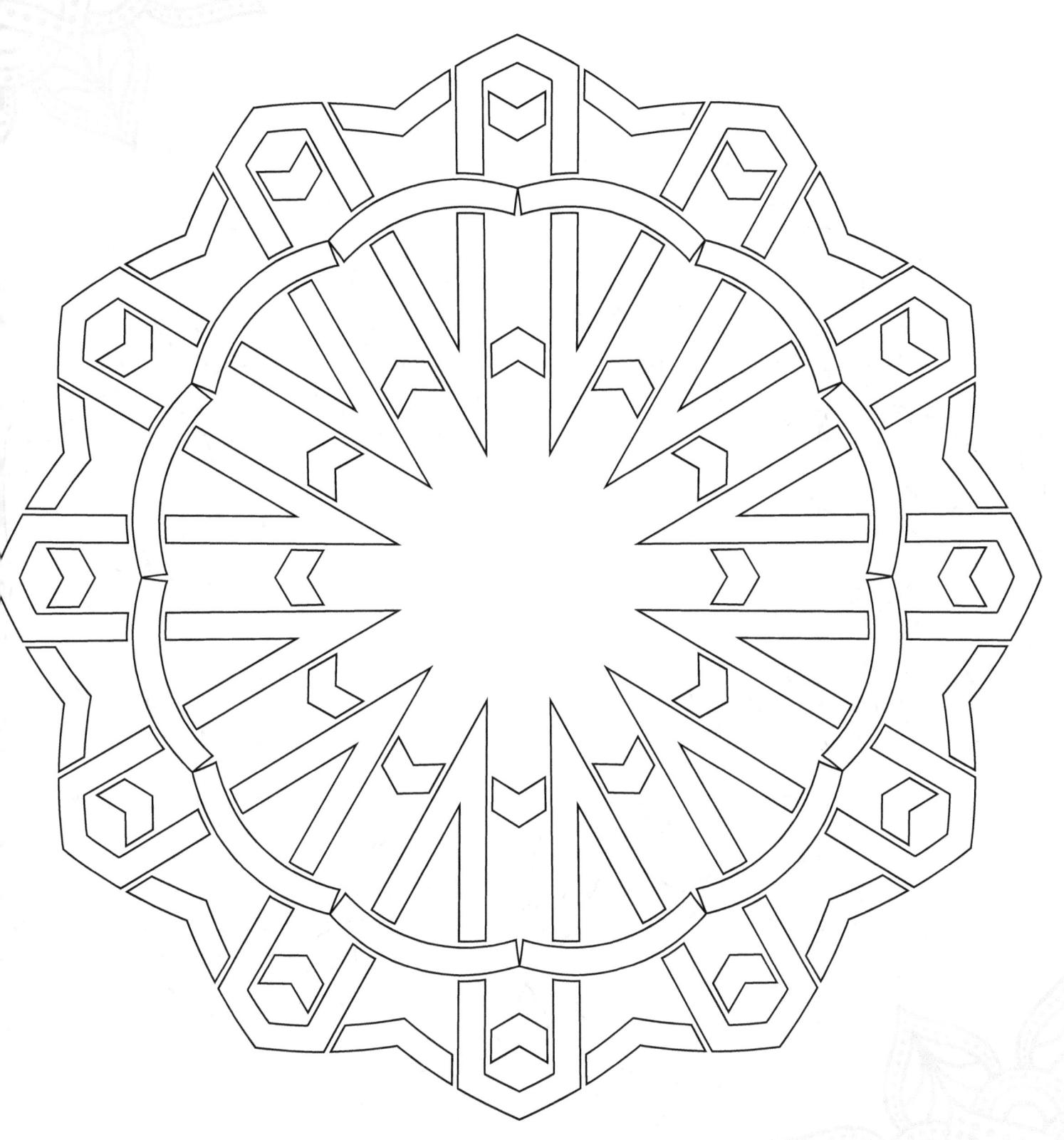

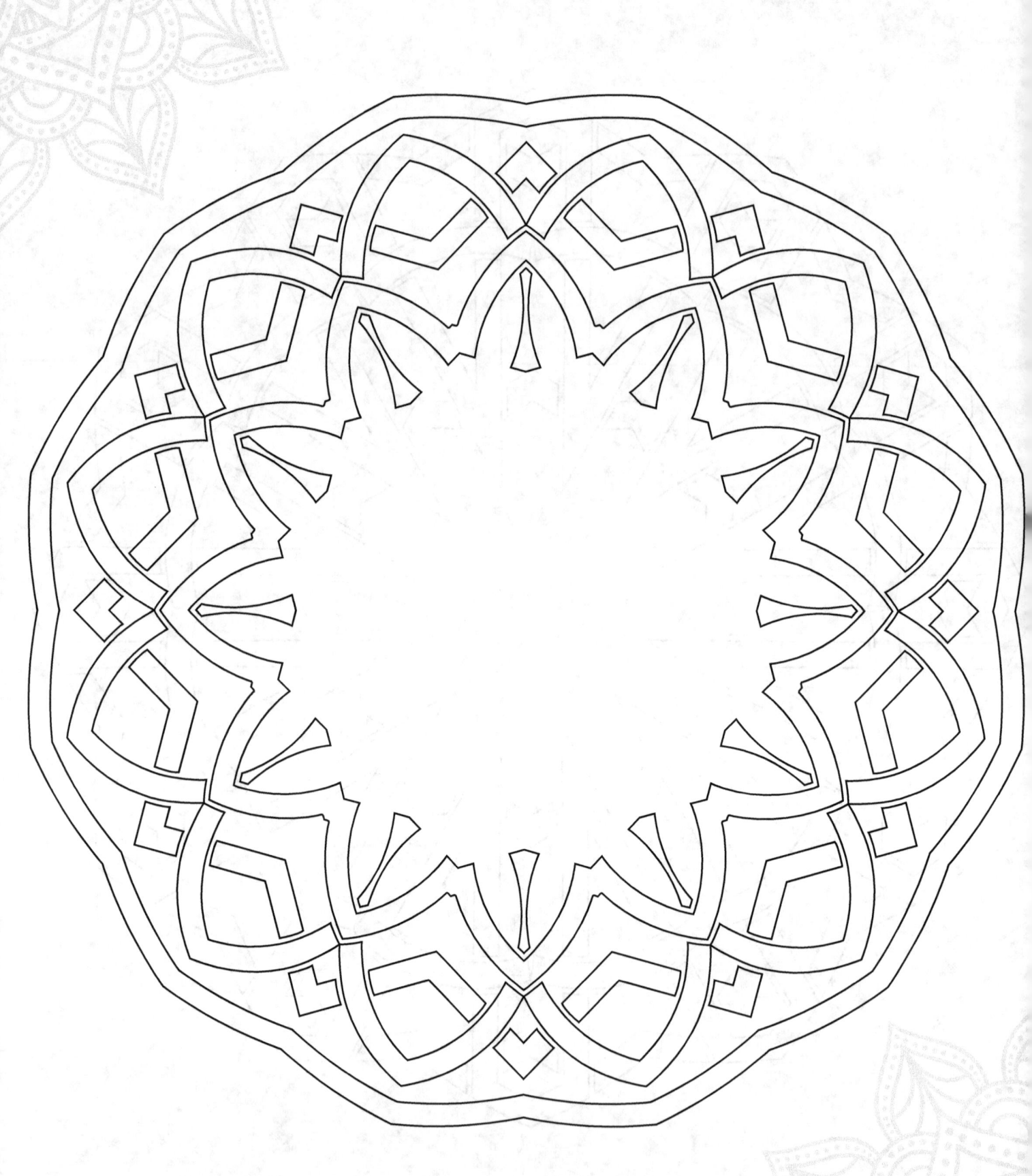

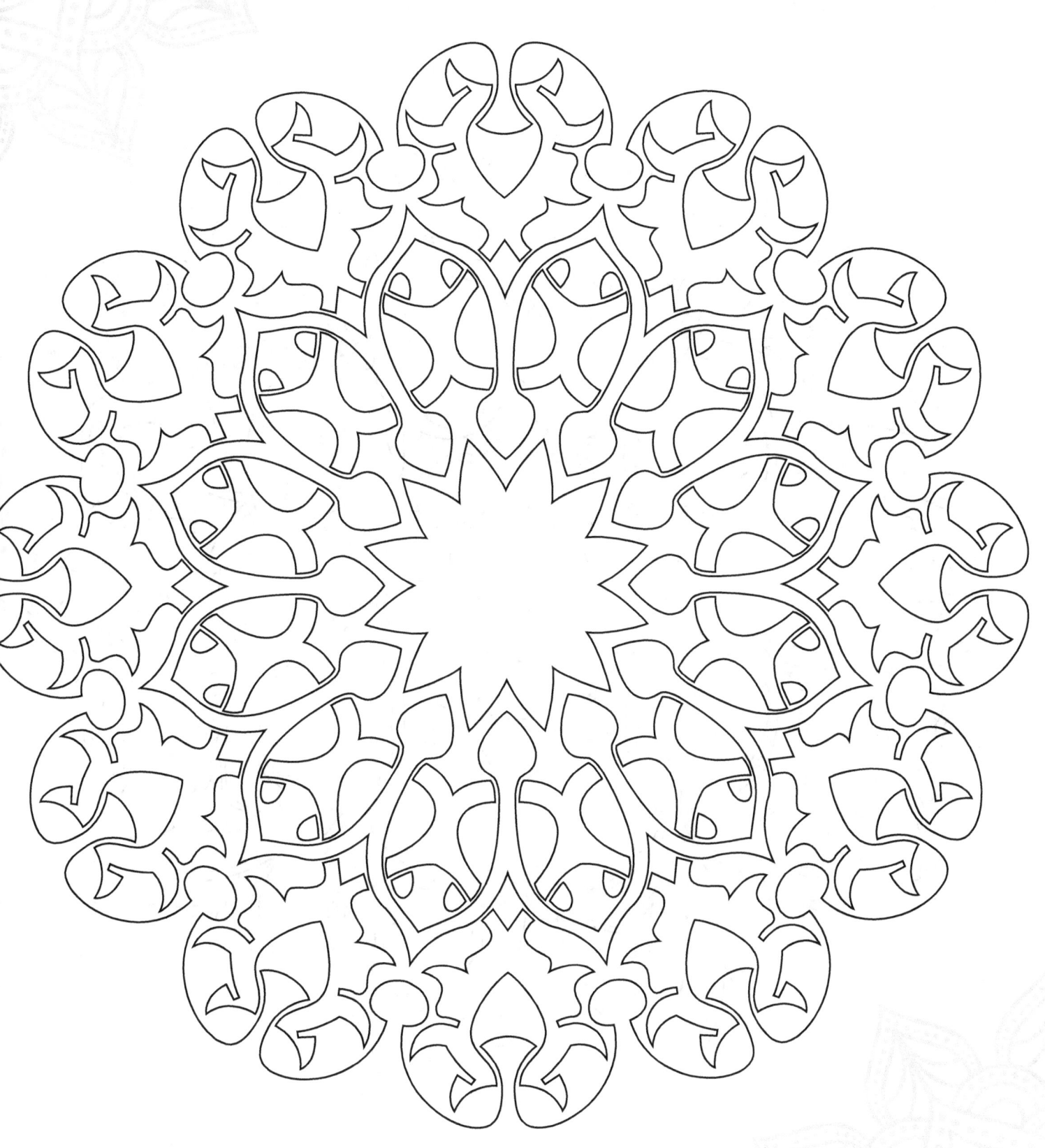

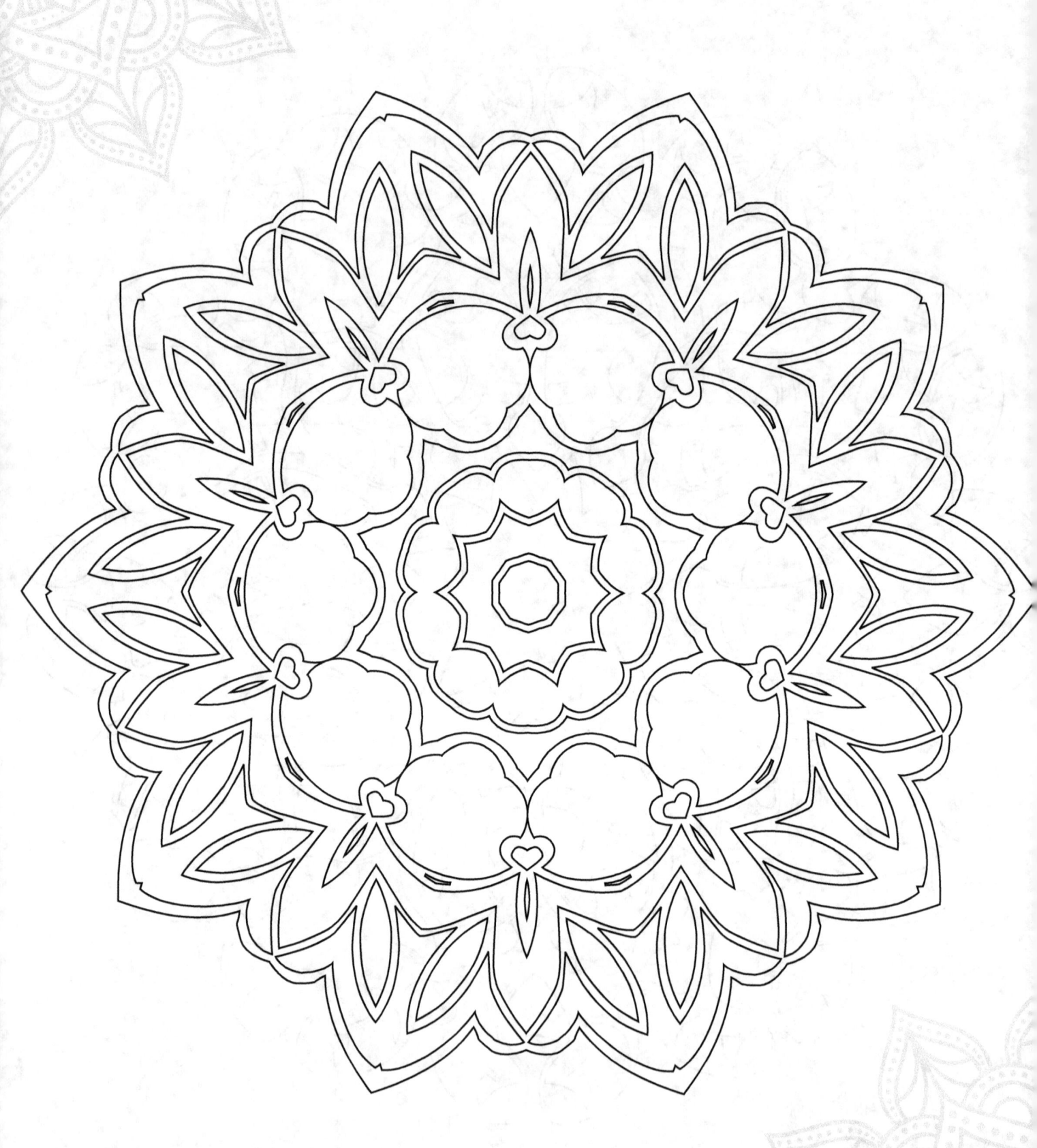

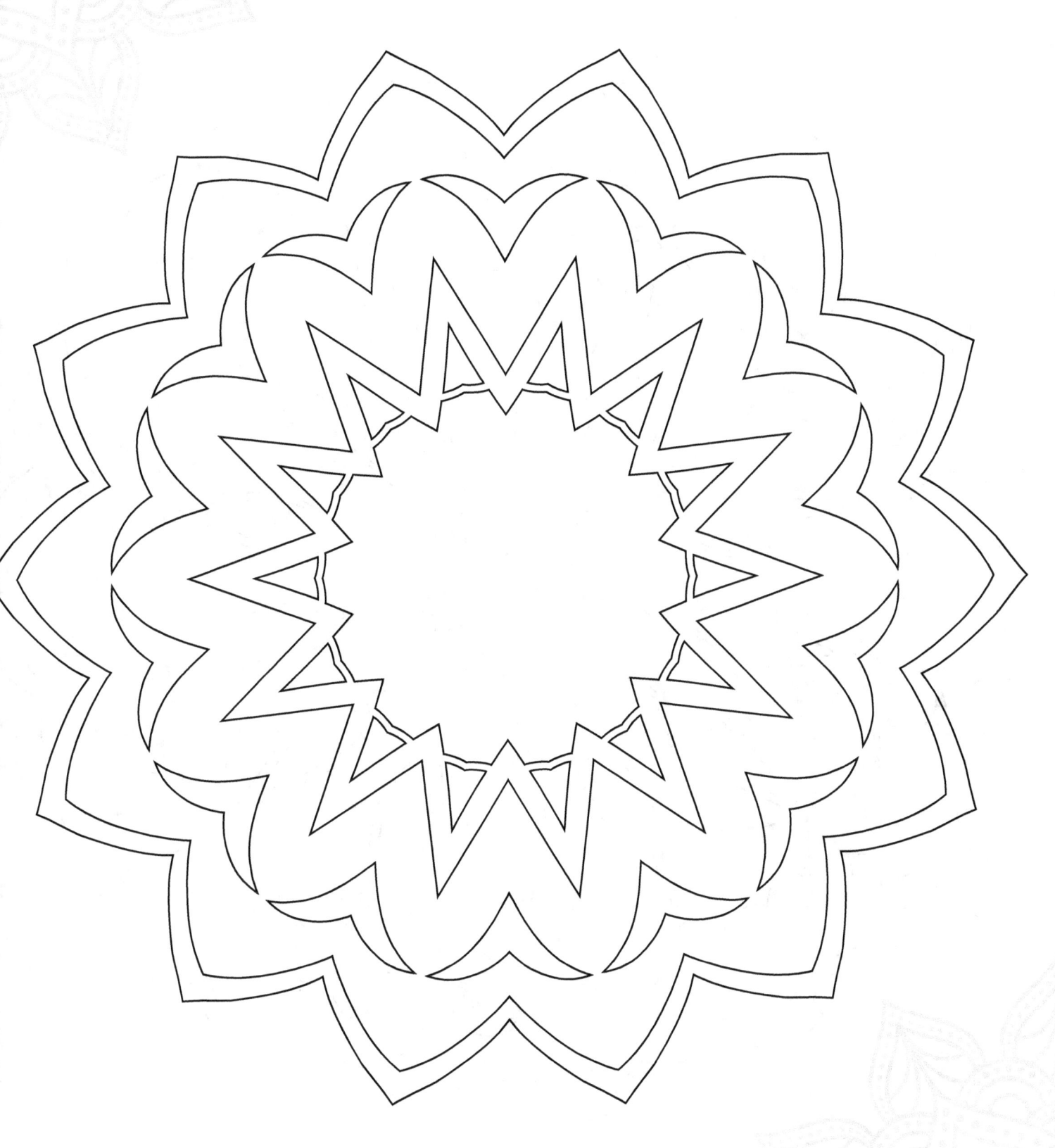

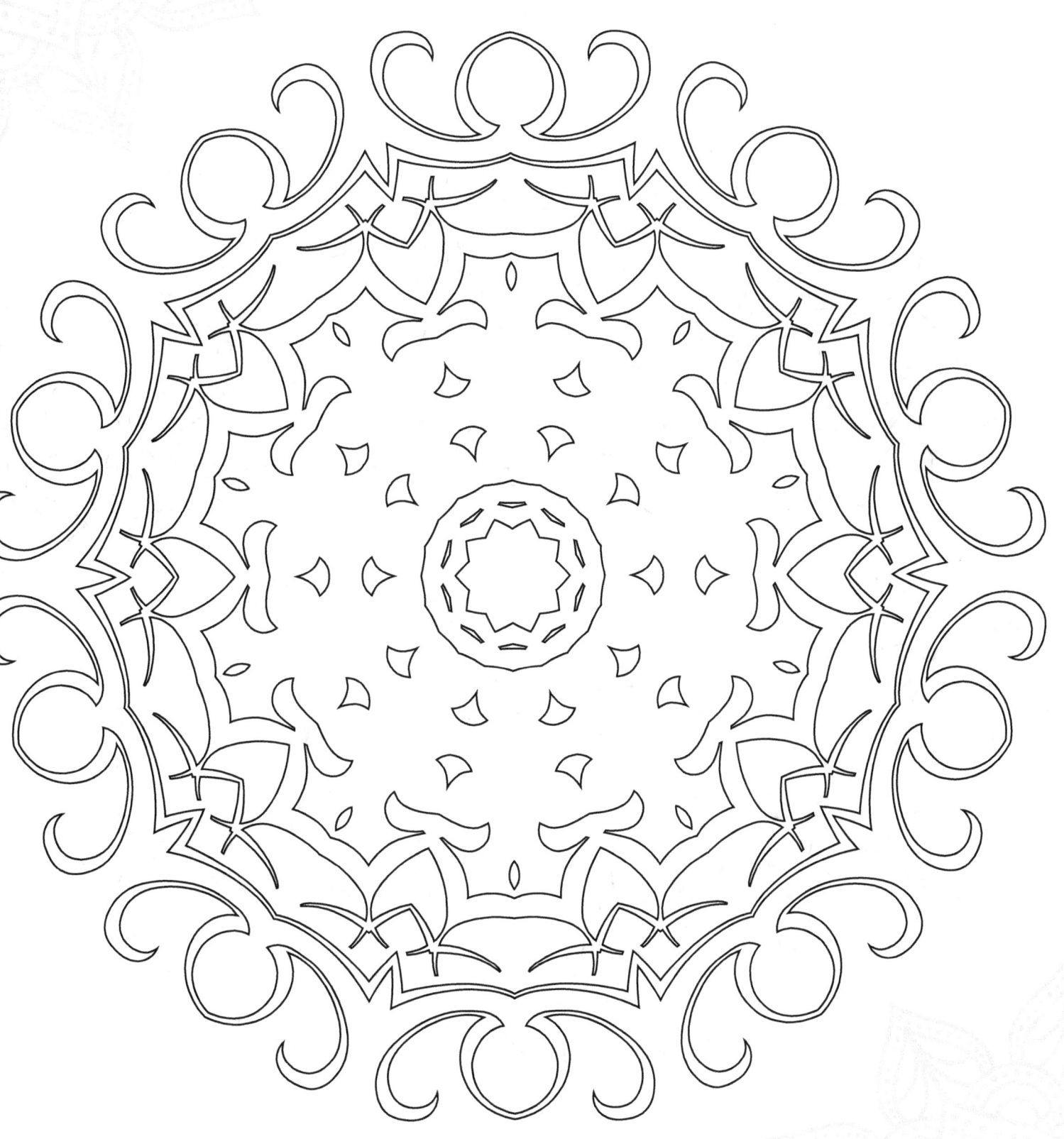

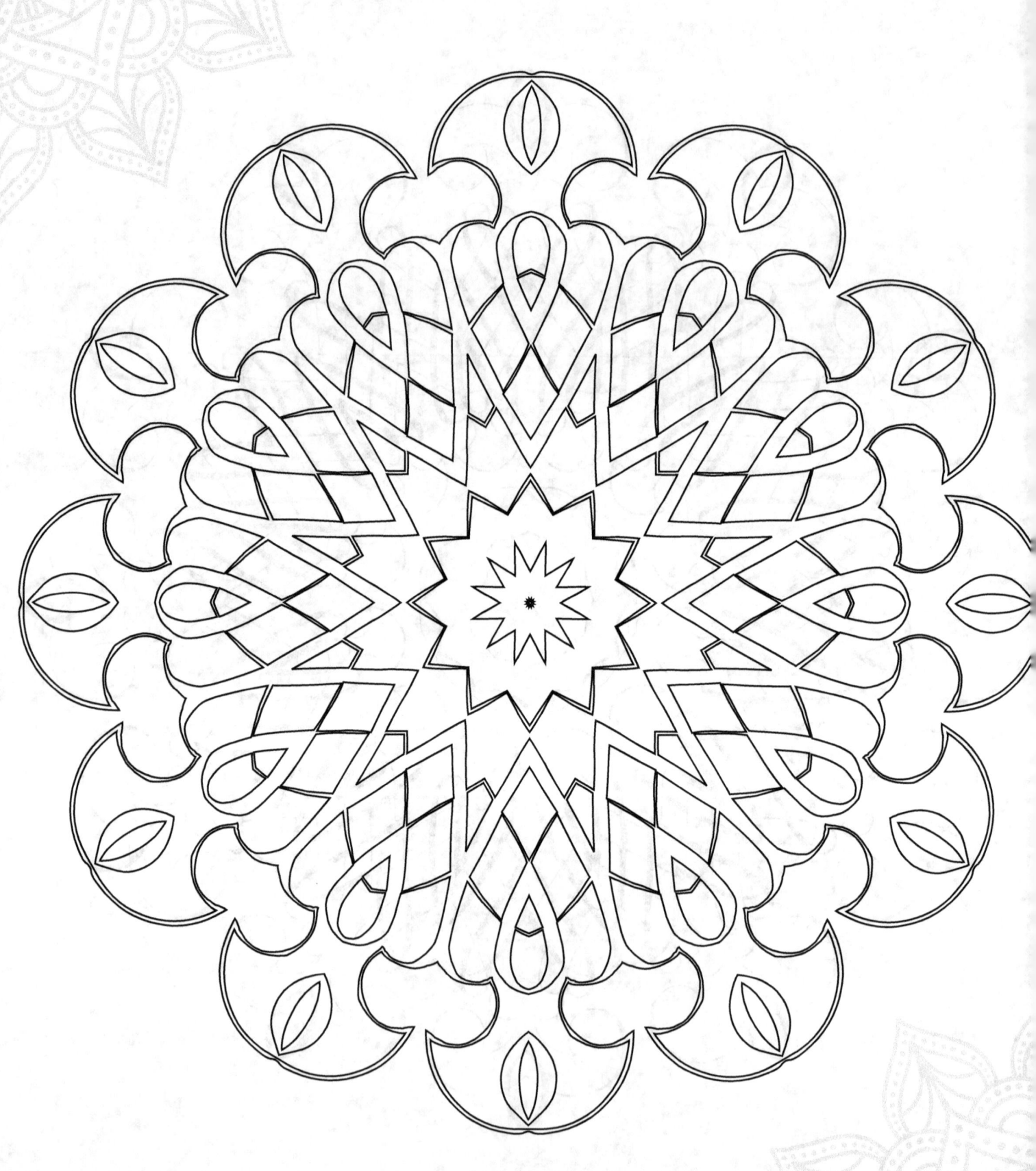

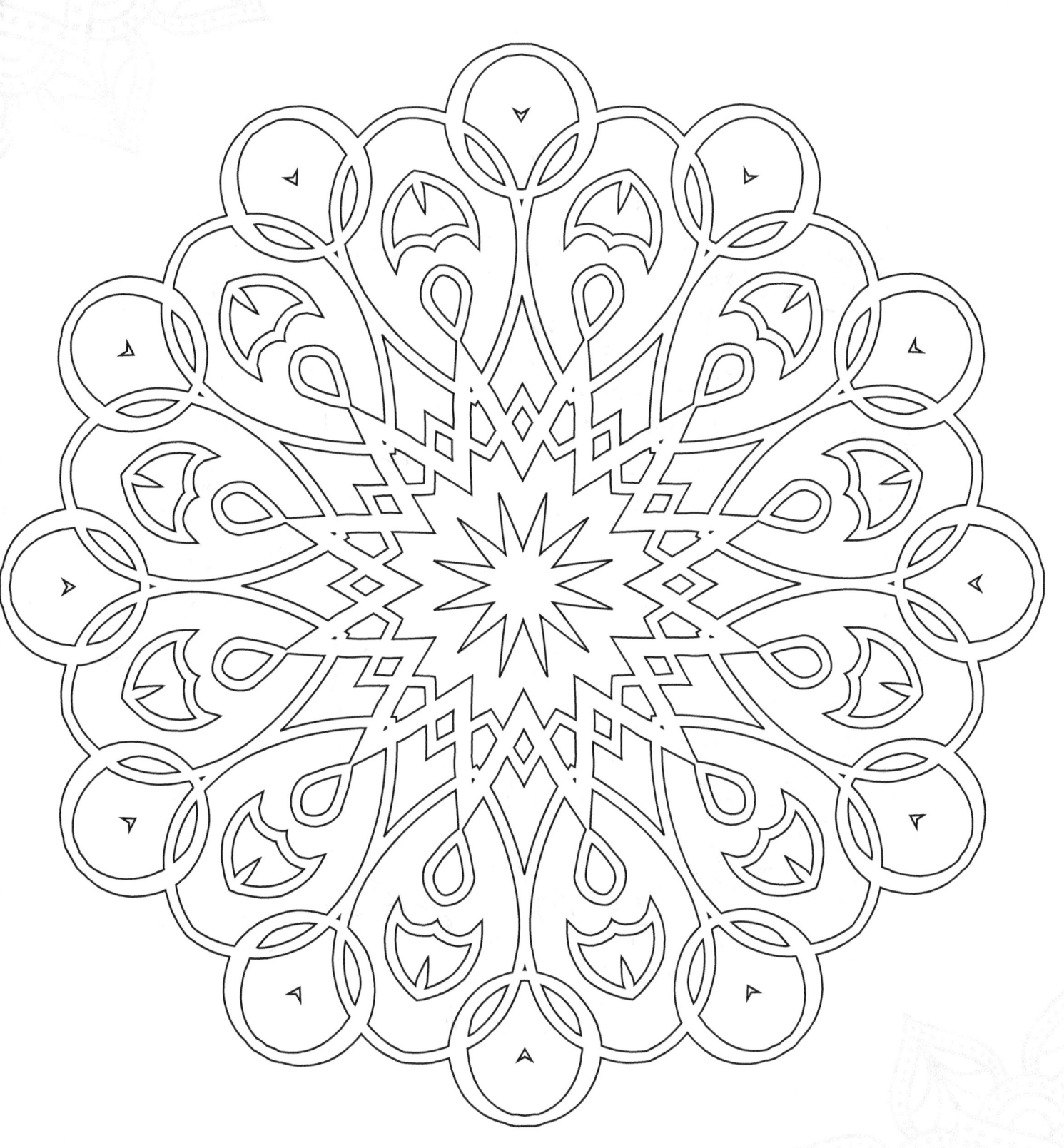

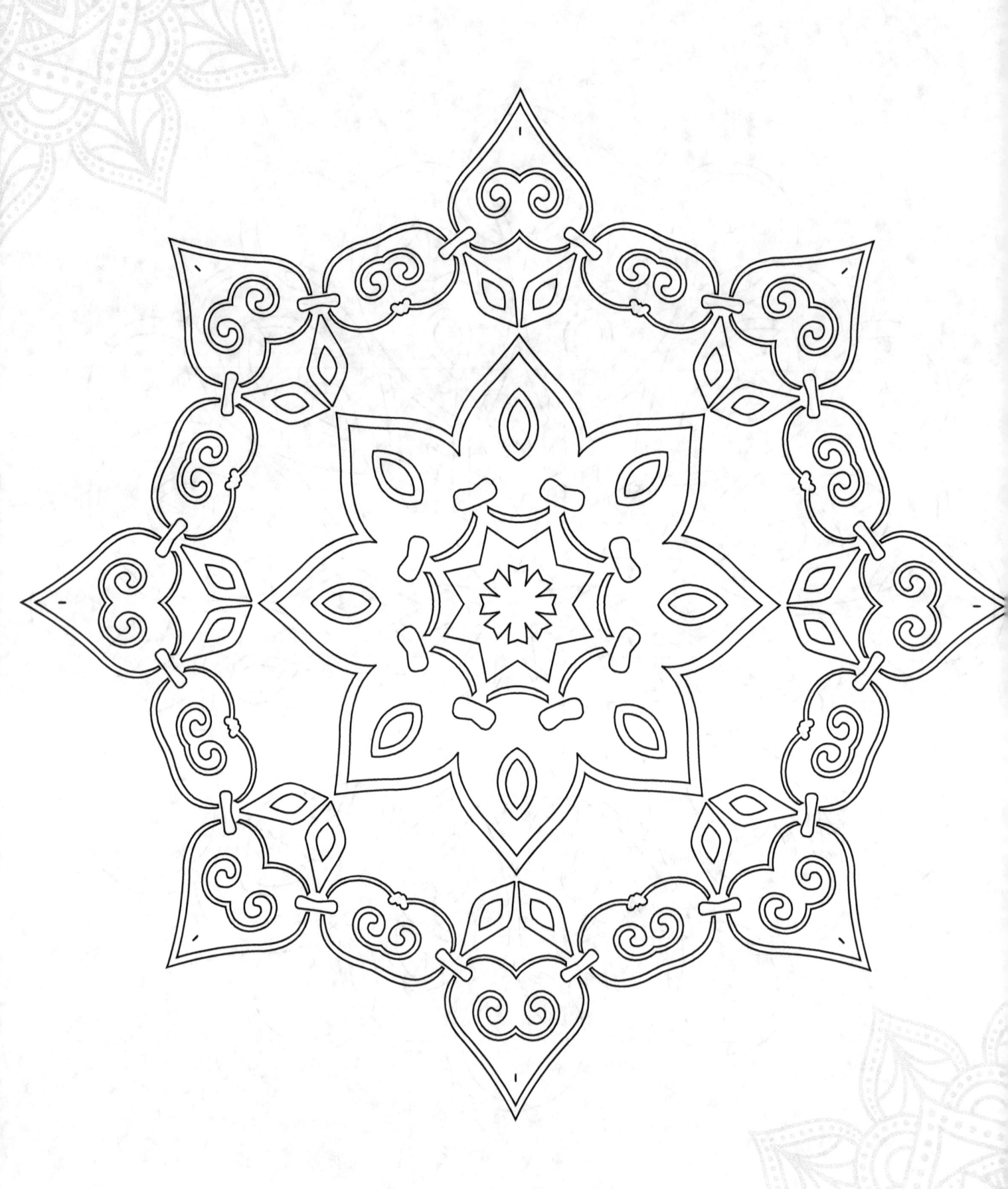

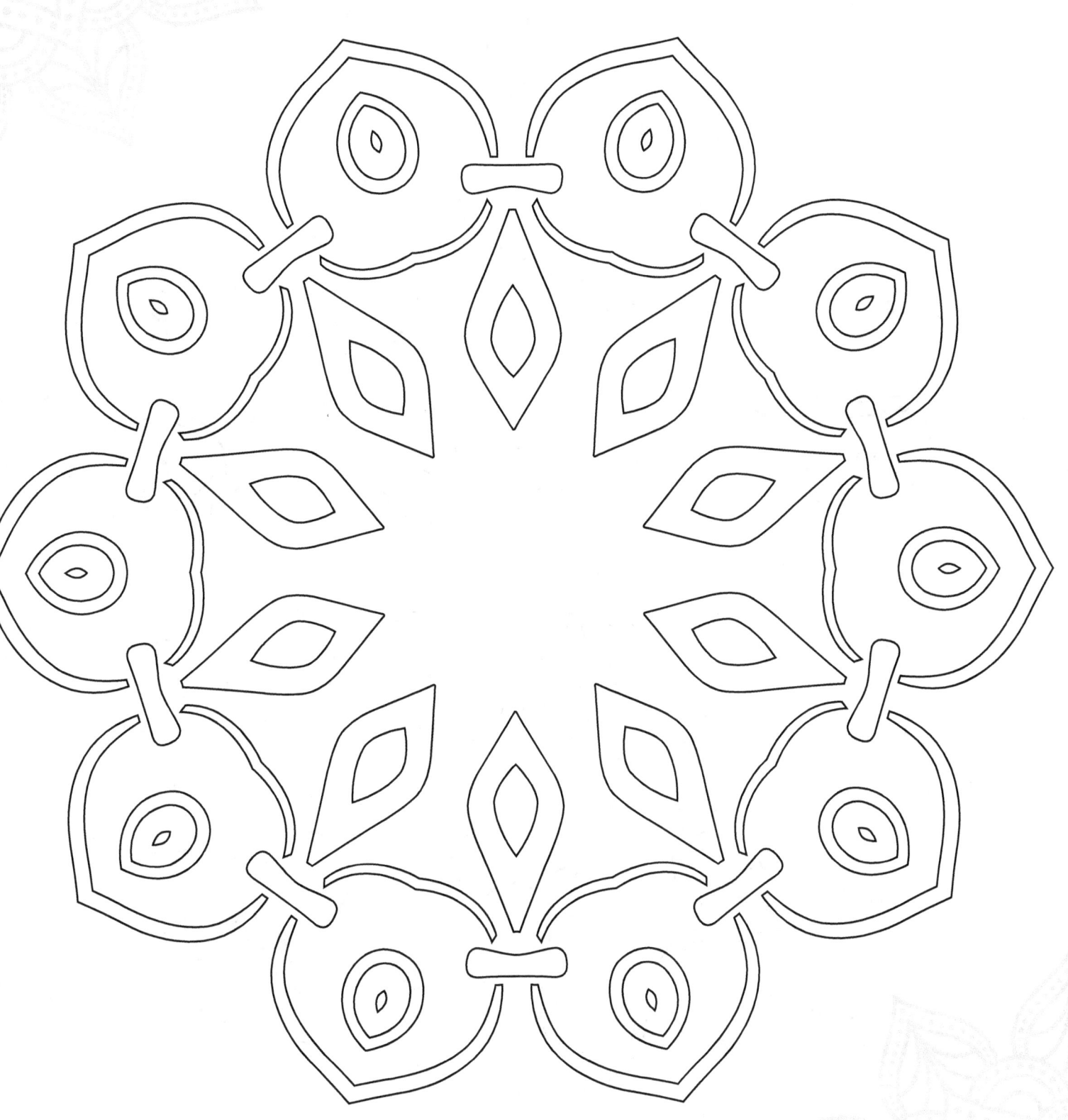

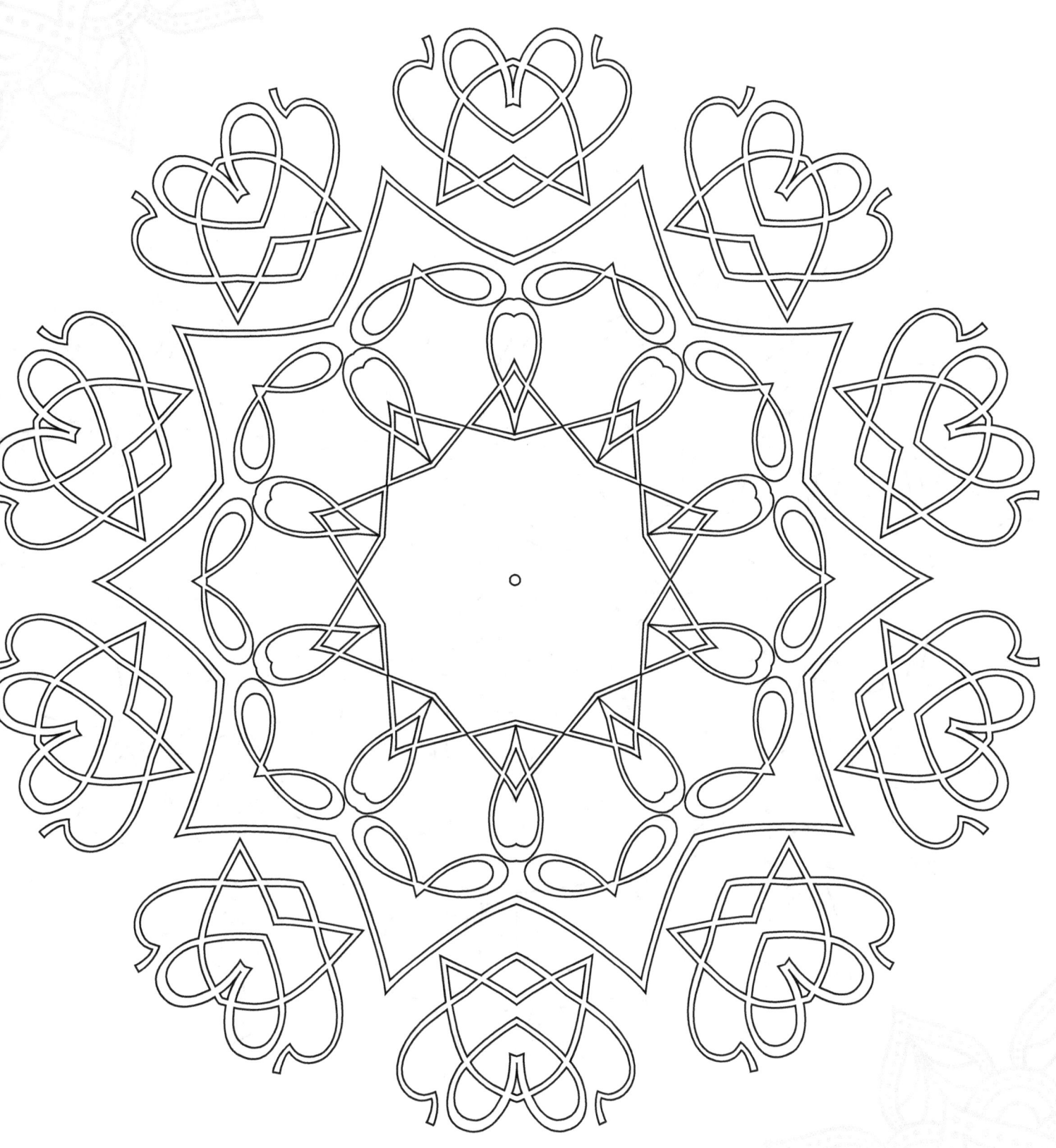

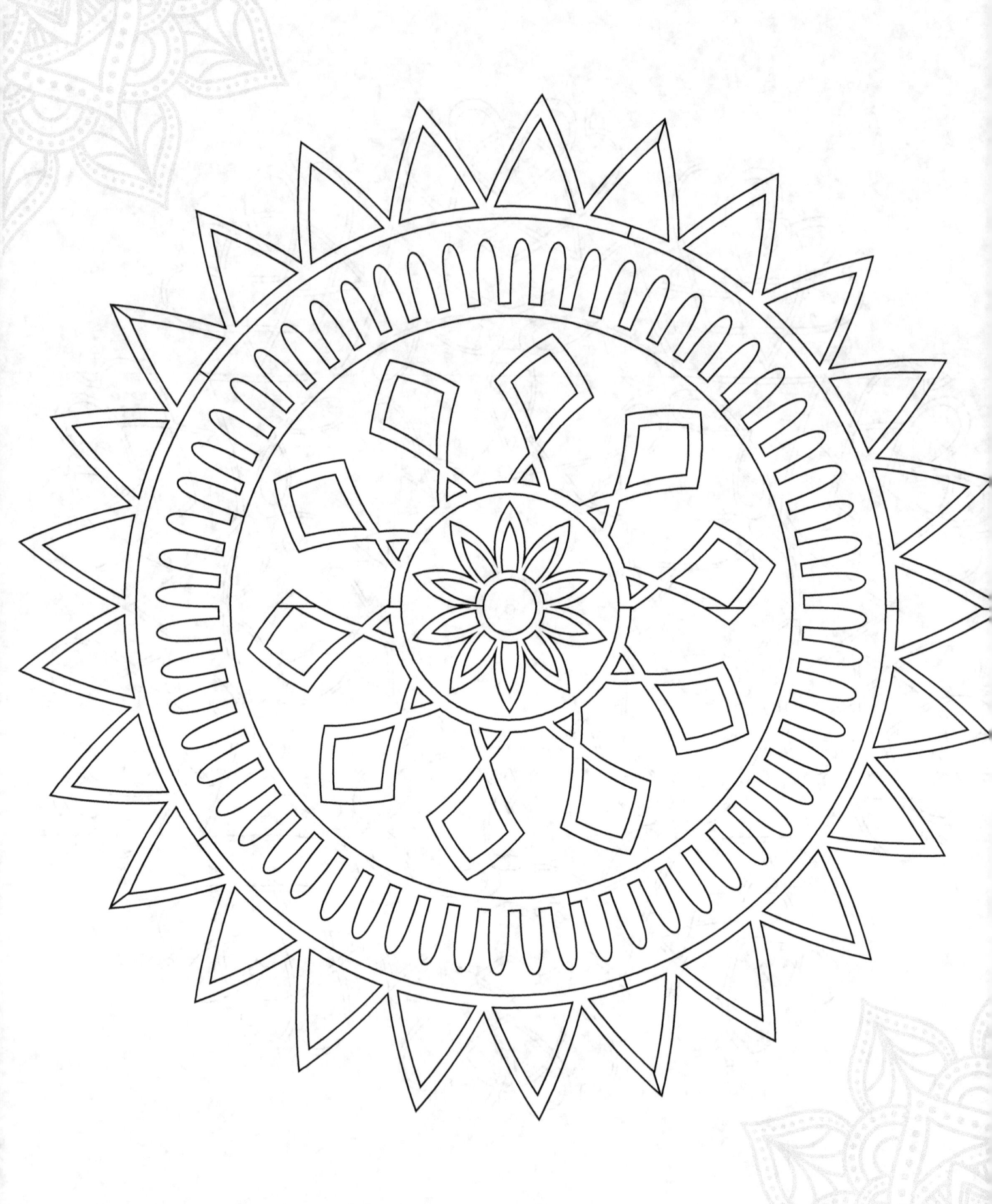

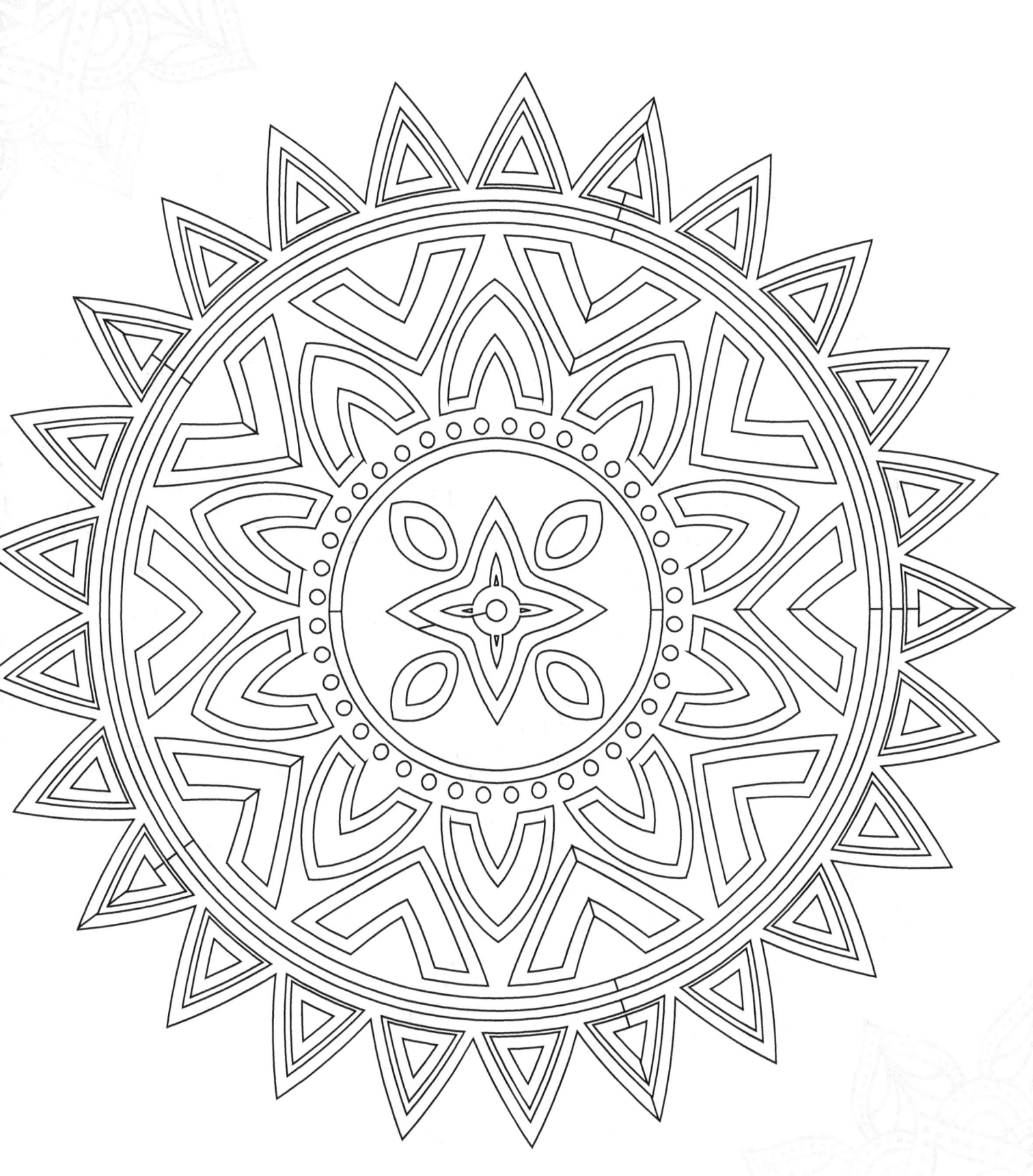

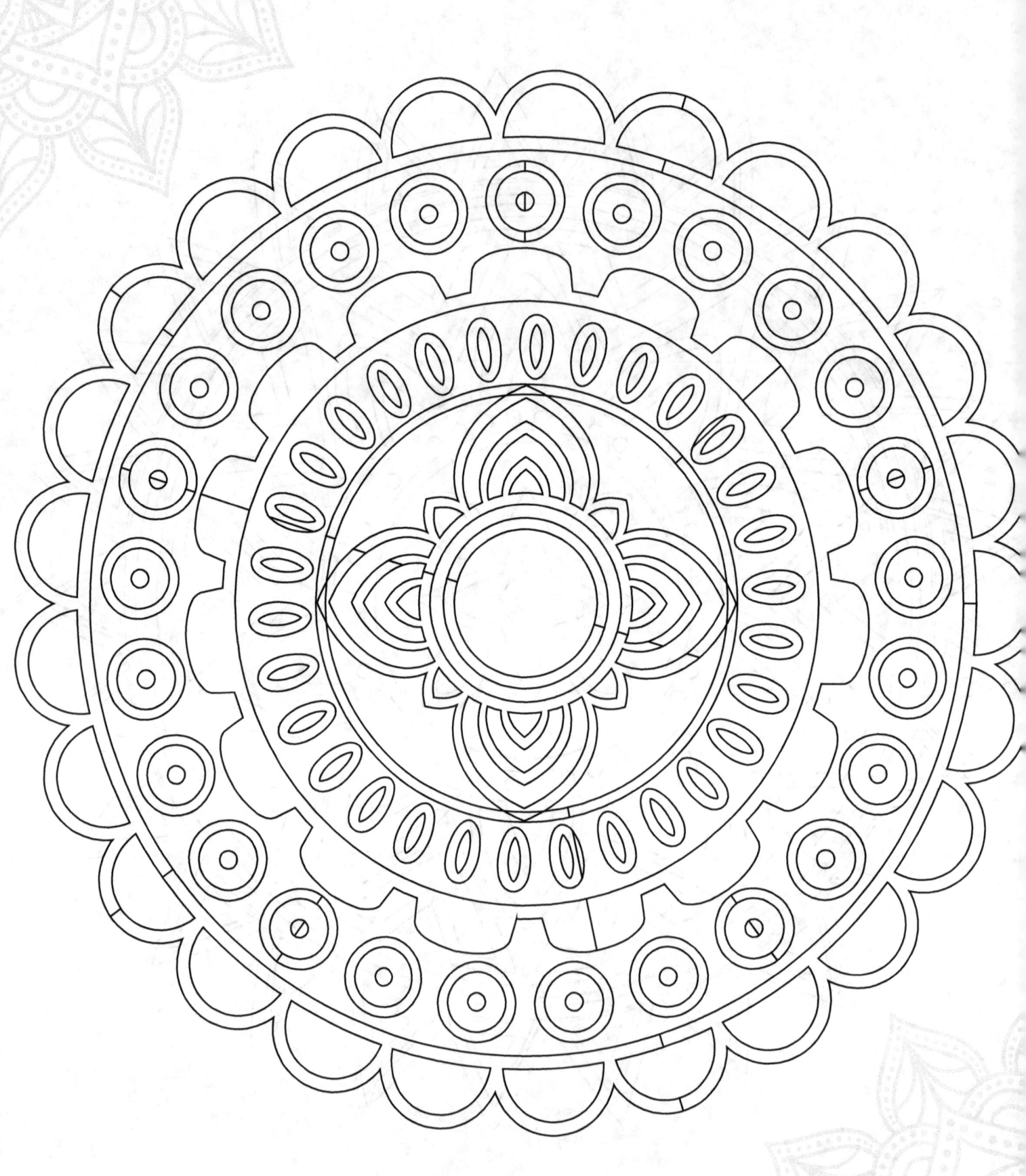

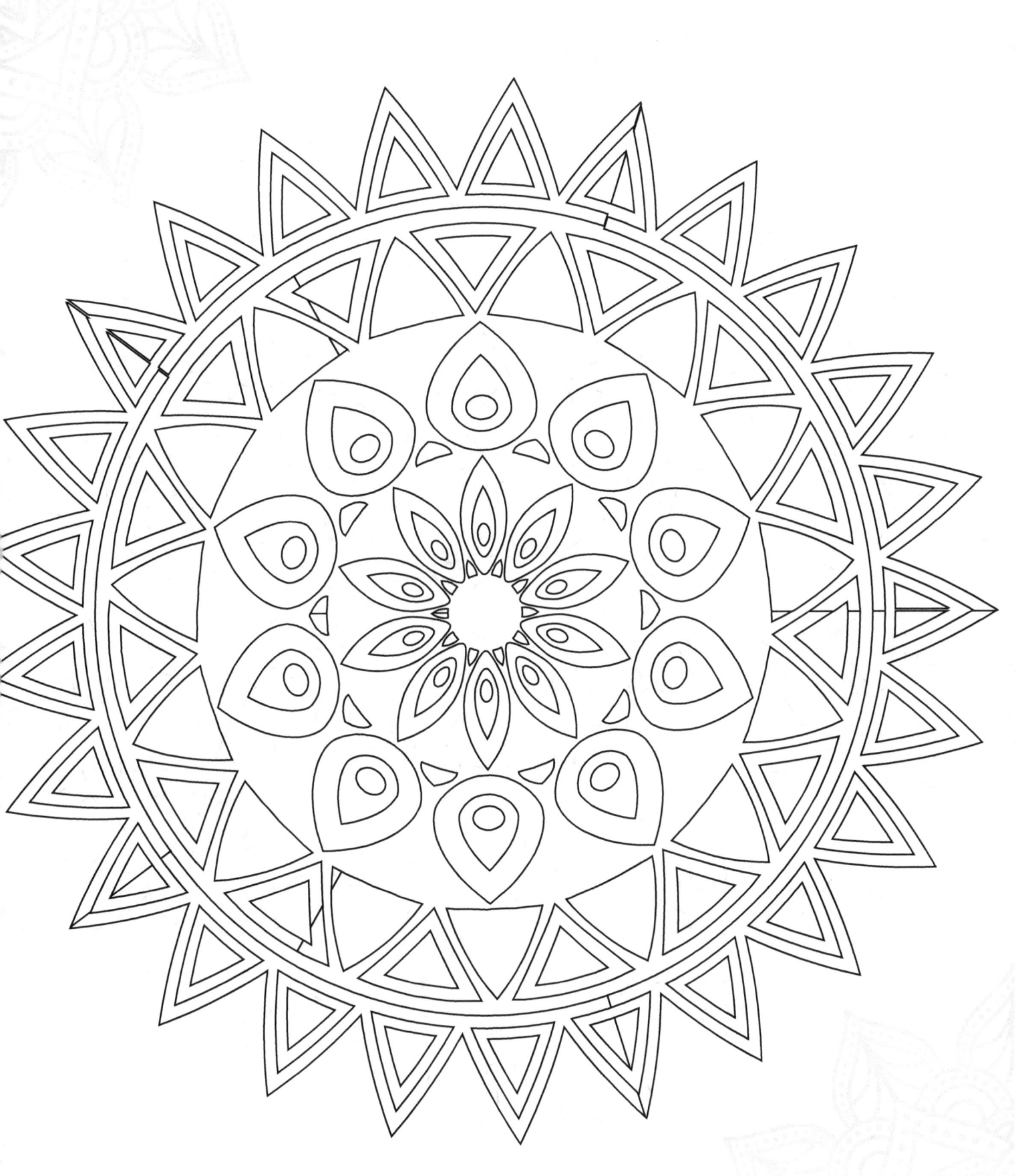

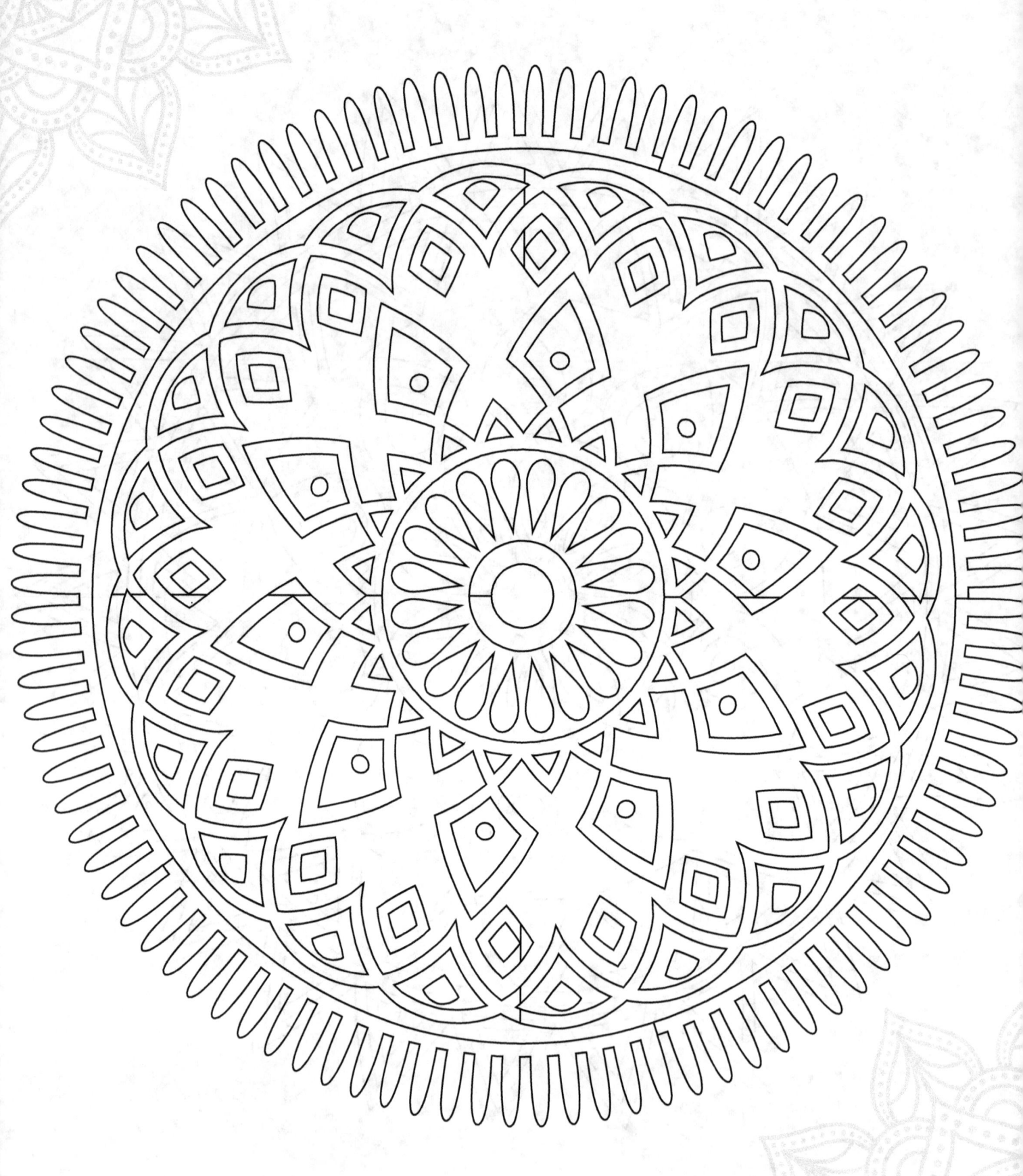

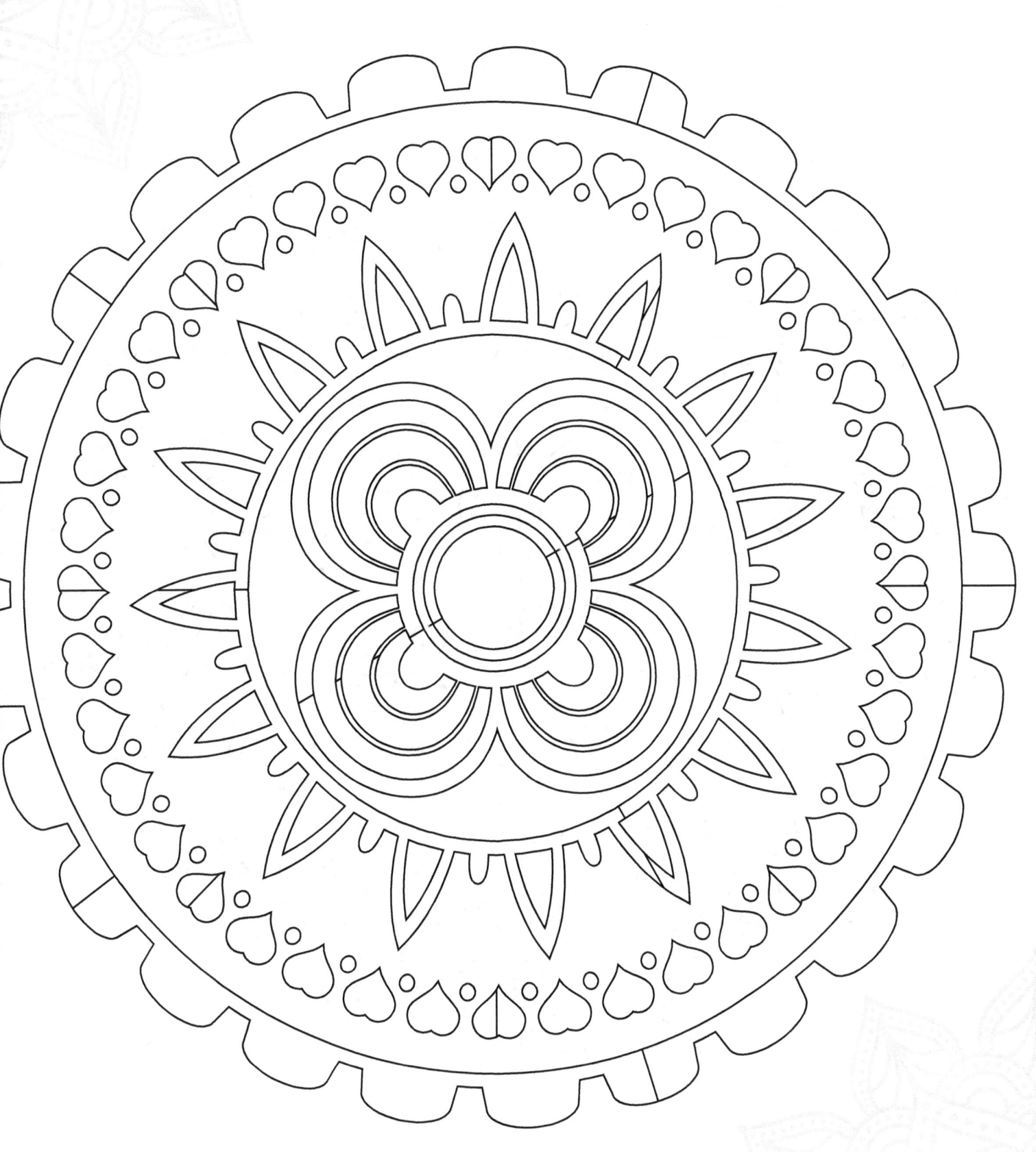

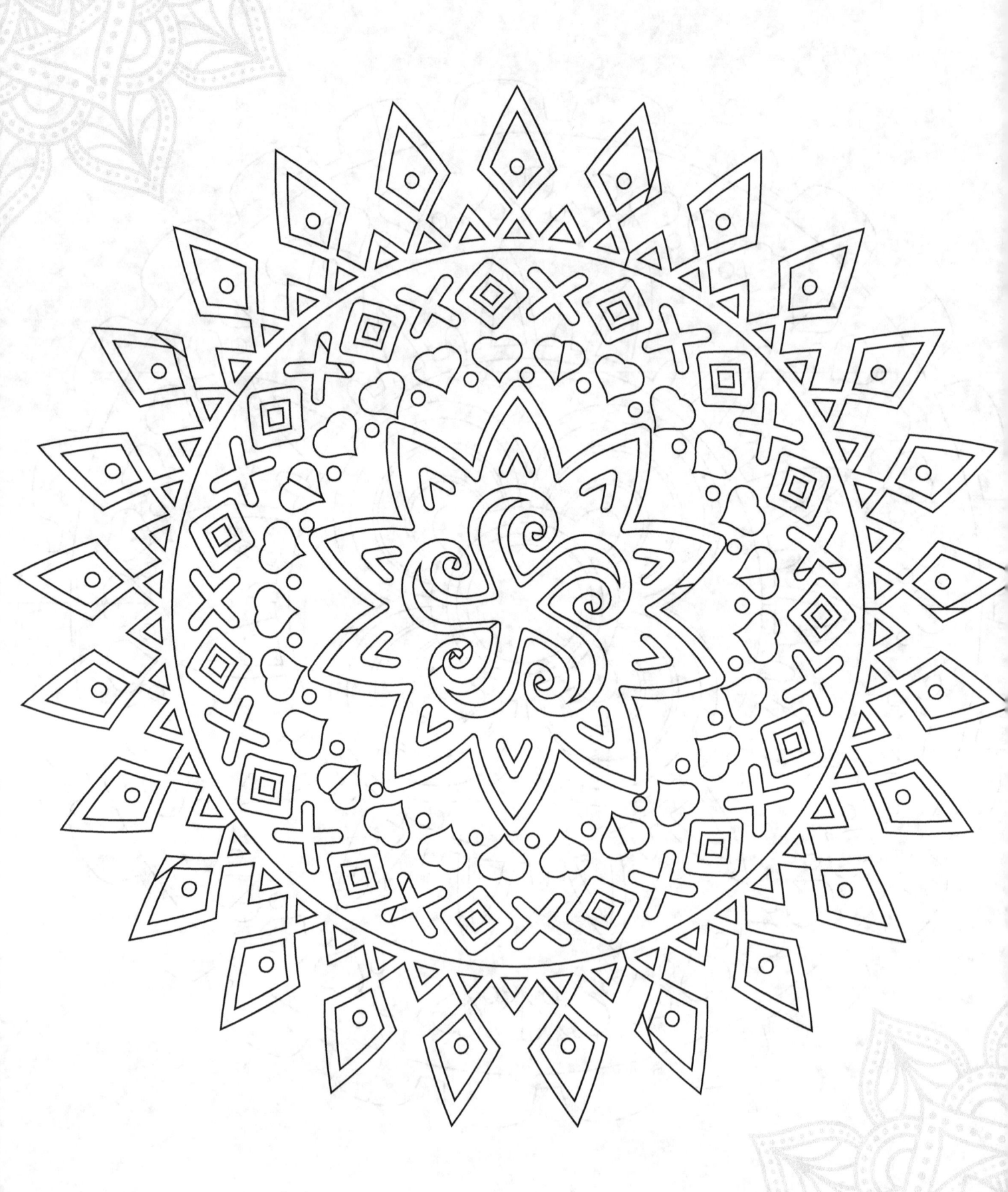

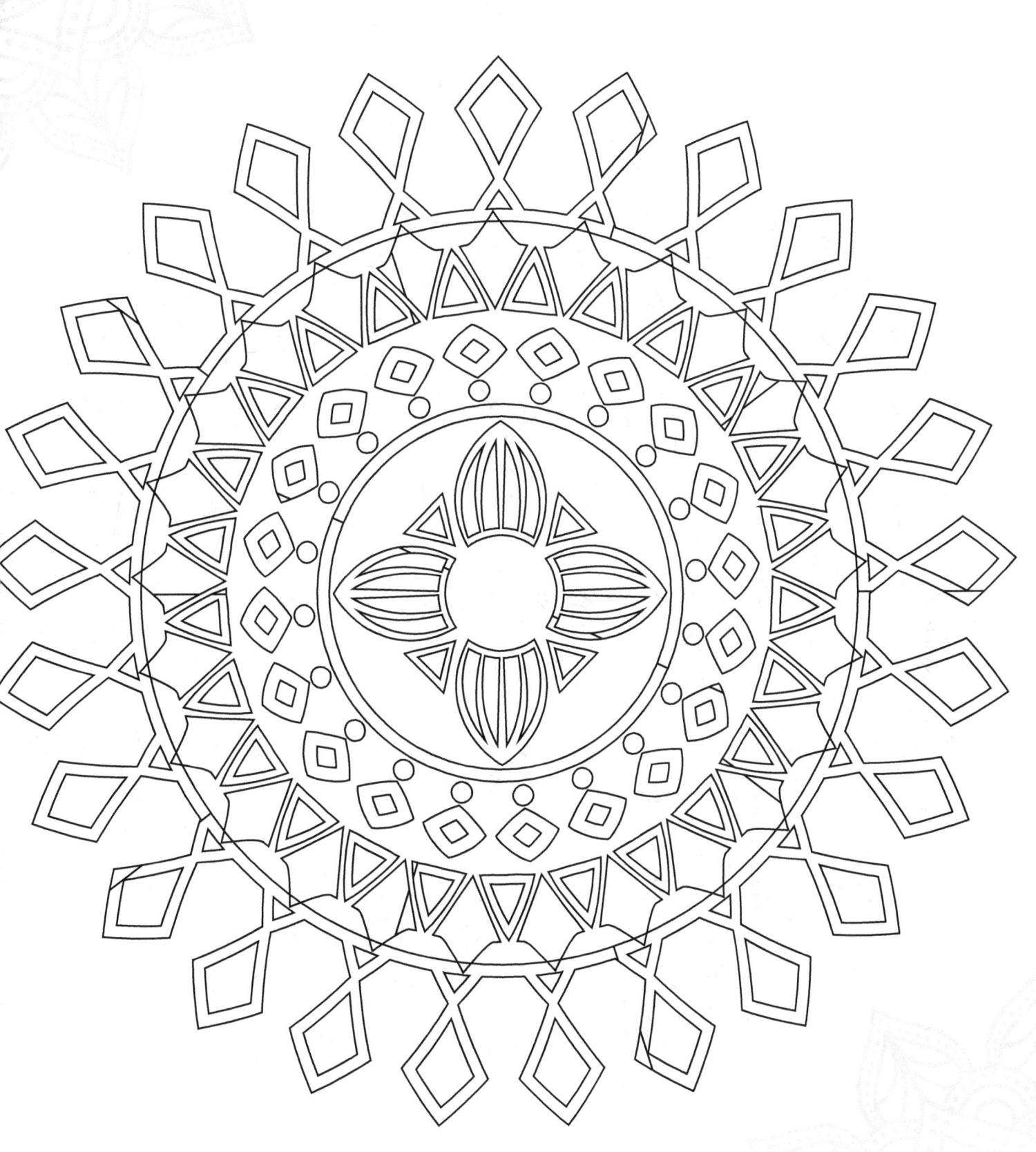

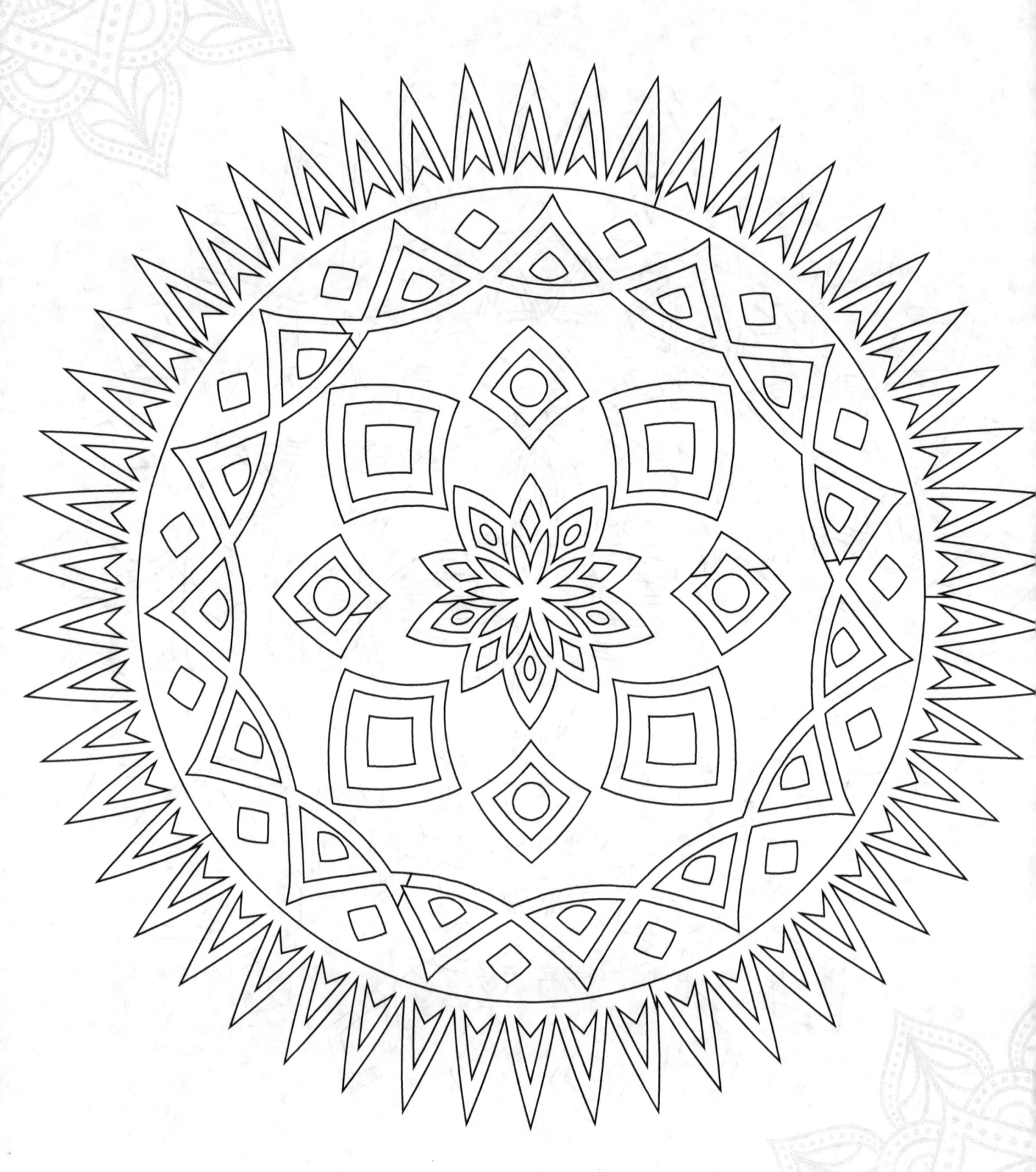

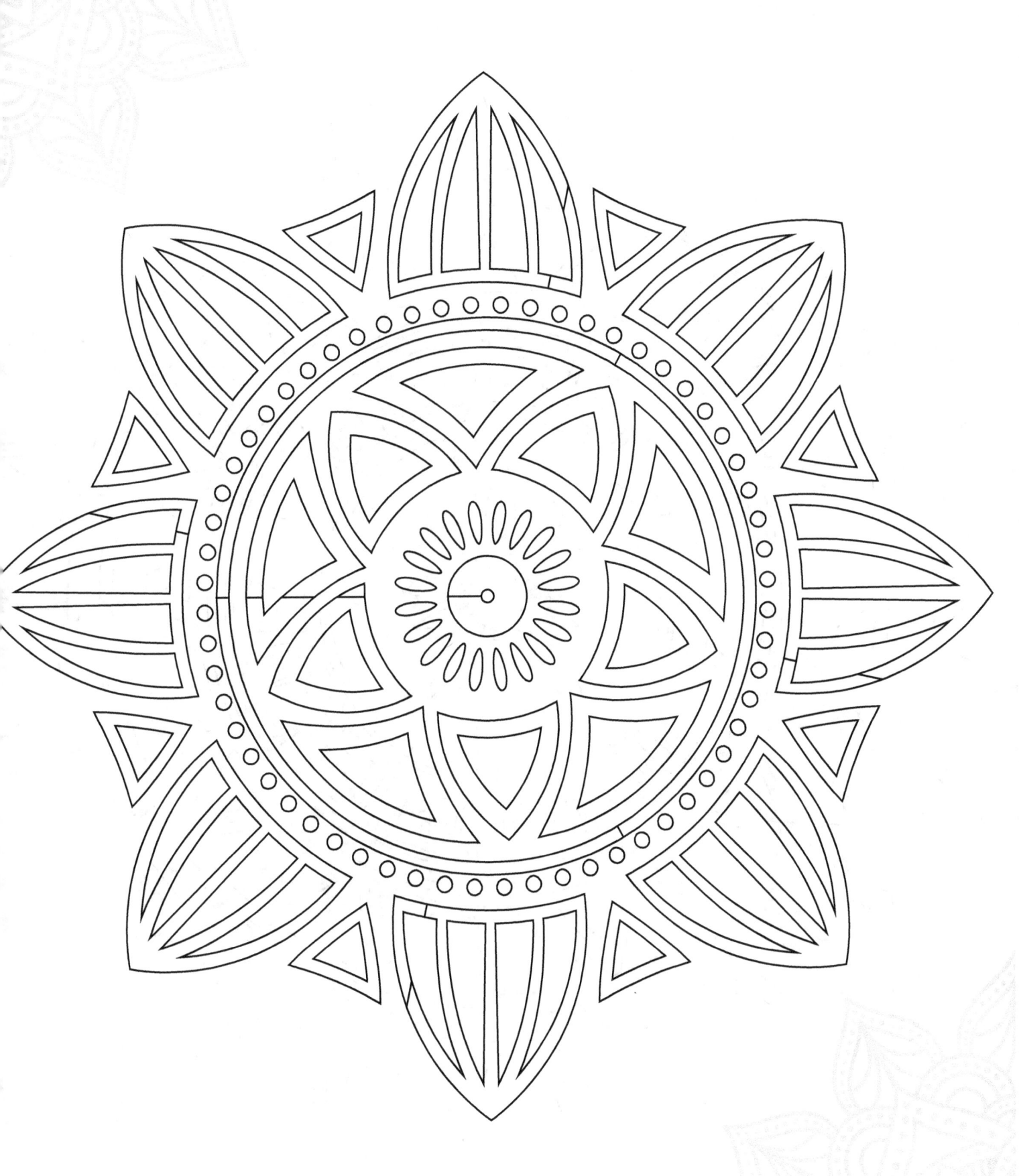

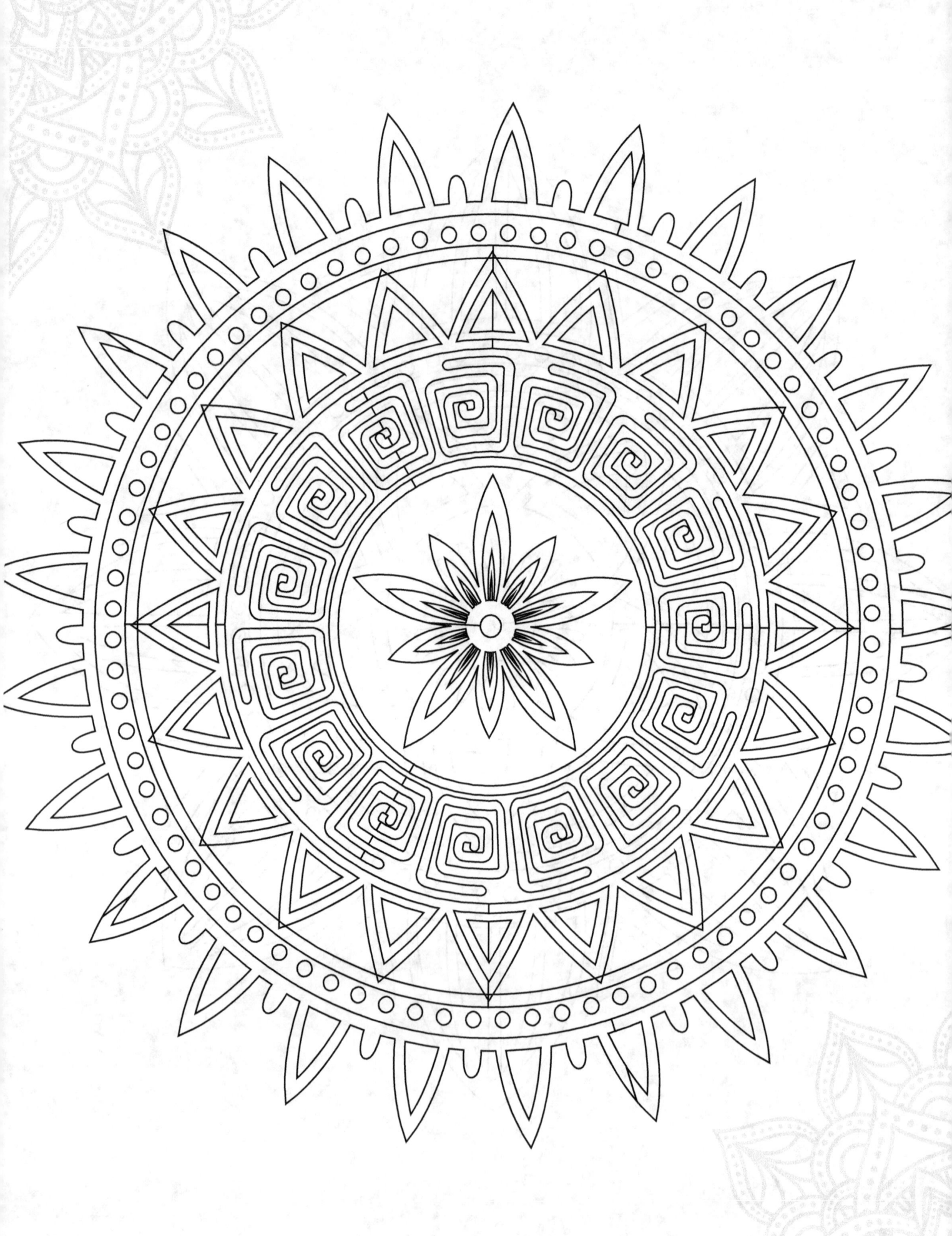

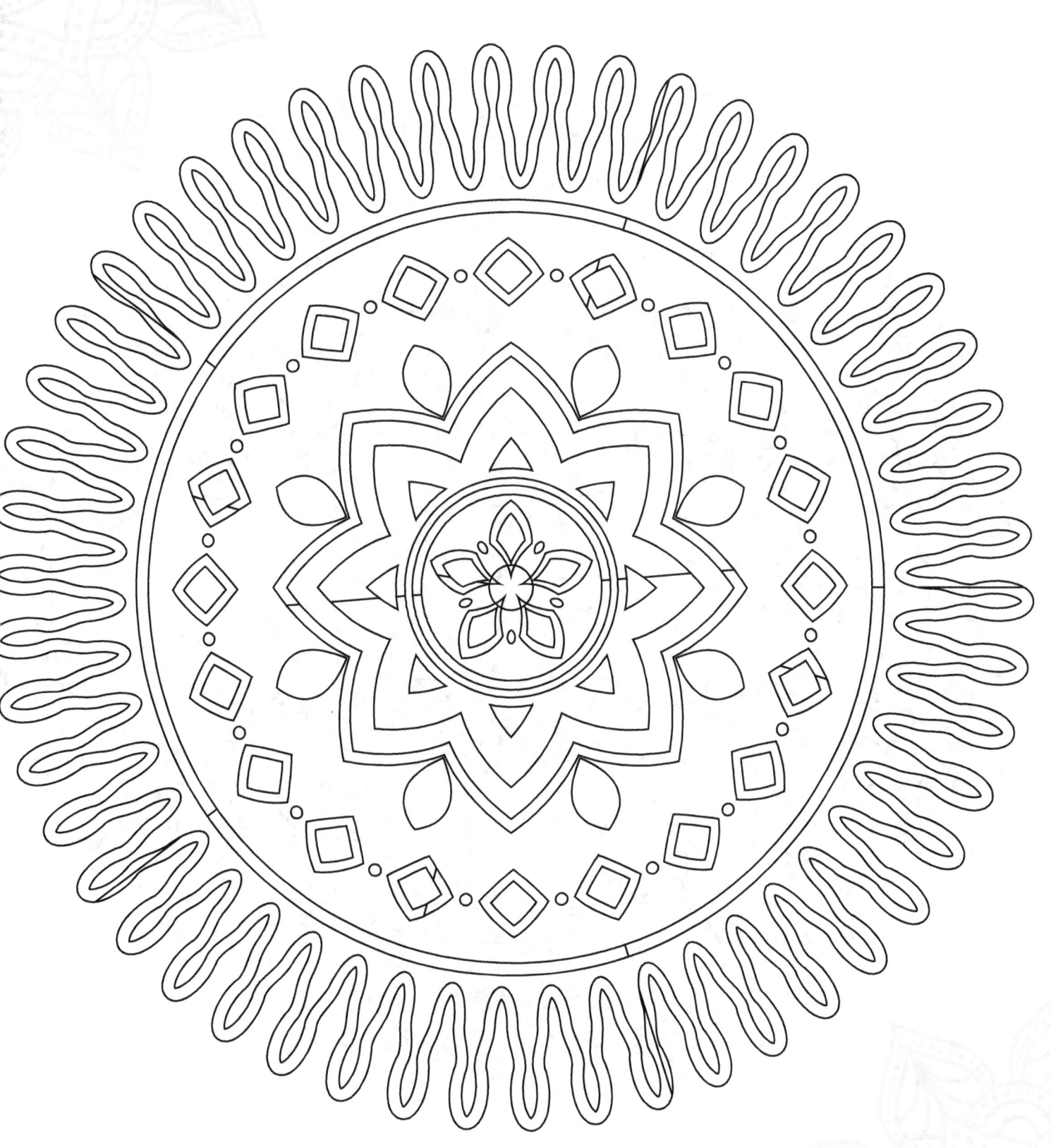

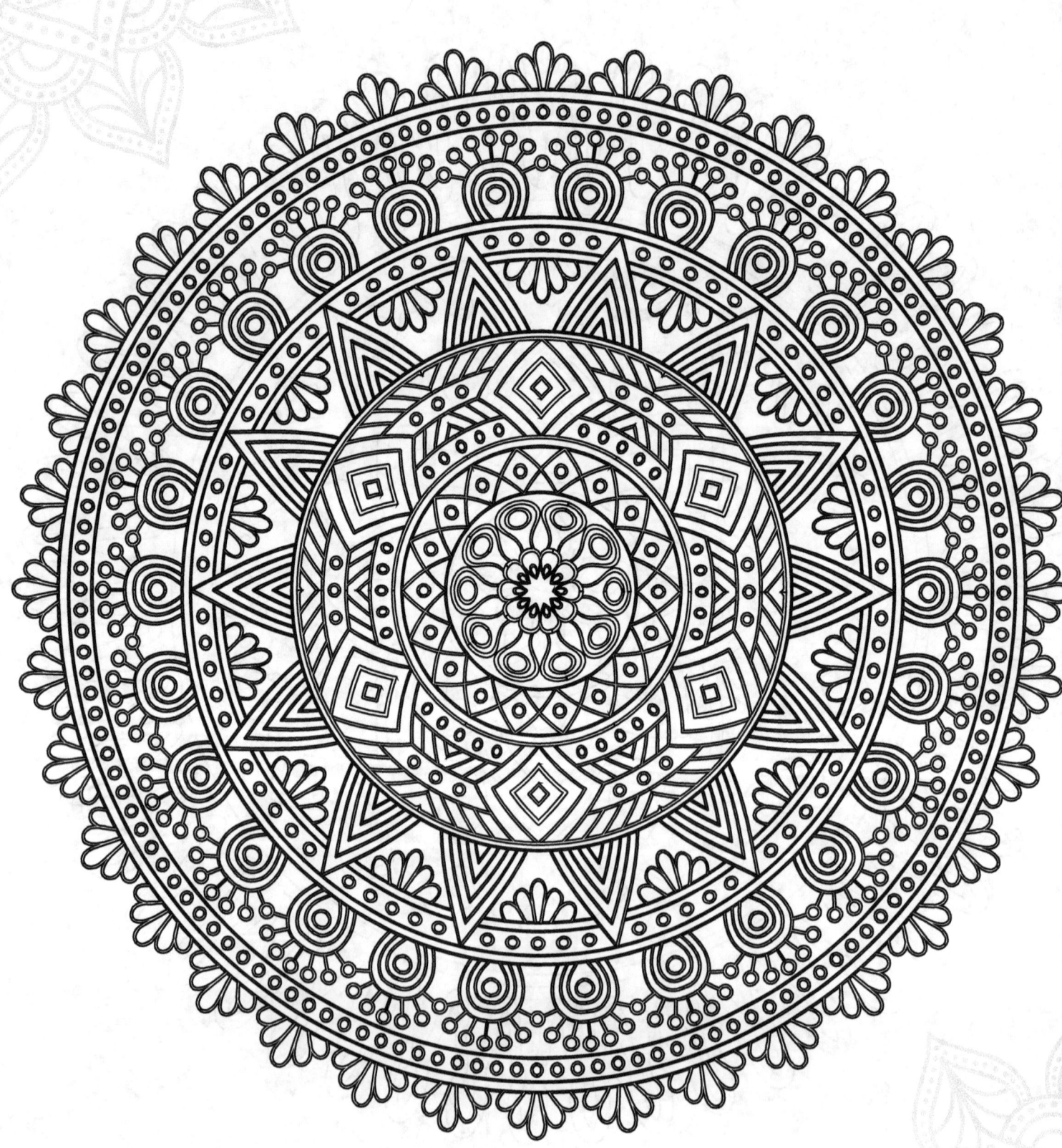

www.ingramcontent.com/pod-product-compliance
Lightning Source LLC
Chambersburg PA
CBHW060423220526
45465CB00008B/2988